BUT GOD

BUT GOD

A story of a broken marriage redeemed through deliverance

Anna Luke

ACKNOWLEDGMENTS

To my sweet Jesus, who has never left my side—to you alone be all the glory. Several years ago during my prayer time, I felt like the Lord told me I was to write a book and call it *But God,* based on Genesis 50:20: "You intended to harm me, but God intended it all for good. He brought me to this position so I could save the lives of many people." Minutes later, my husband walked into the room and said, "I feel like God has given me a word for you. You are to write a book telling our story and call it *But God.*" That weekend, two other people who knew nothing of this came up to me with the same message that I was to write a book. Thank you, Jesus, for providing every step of the way.

I would like to thank my husband, who ever since God freed him has boldly told me to share ANY detail of our life in hopes that others will also be set free. I am so grateful for you, my love.

To my sweet editor who will remain nameless, there are not enough words to express my thanks to you! The readers will never know, this side of heaven, how many of these :) (emojis) you saved them from, but I know, and I thank you. Per our agreement of disposing of the rest, I get to keep just that one as a reminder of all our time together. (You thought I forgot.) You are such a treasure.

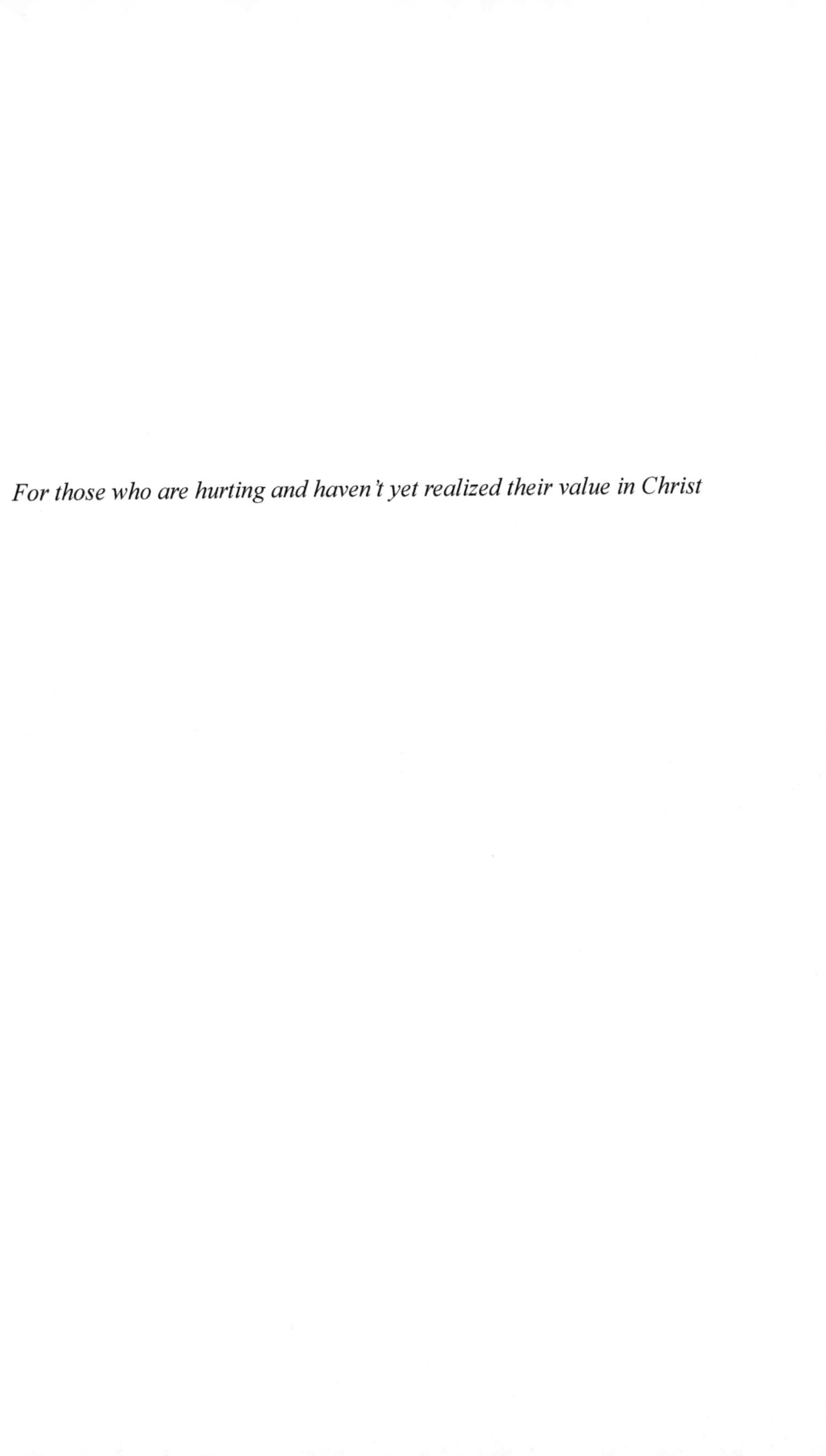

For those who are hurting and haven't yet realized their value in Christ

CONTENTS

1

OBEDIENCE

"Never be afraid to trust an unknown future to a known God."

CORRIE TEN BOOM

I SHOULD HAVE KEPT my big mouth shut. Over breakfast one morning, I told my friend Eugene (who goes to Iraq frequently) to please tell the women and young girls who had escaped ISIS that there is a momma who loves them dearly and prays for them every day. At this point, I had already had a bake sale and yard sale to raise money for them, with even more fundraising planned. Because I am content being a geographically long-distance helper, I think he missed the part of my sentence where I said, "You go tell them." His reply was unsettling.

"Anna, why don't you come yourself?"

I explained to him, "I would love to, but you see, I don't have the health for it. I get severe migraines and am in bed sometimes two-plus days a week. And to make things even worse, I'm severely hypoglycemic. I have to eat every hour. I never go anywhere without protein snacks on hand. That, my friend, is why I am called to the American mission field and help the refugees here. You know, where I still get to sleep in my own bed, have my own fridge, and I don't run the risk of starring in an ISIS film."

Why was Eugene staring at me unfazed?

"Anna, we will be able to get you food as often as you like. You should come."

Who does that? Who tells you to still come when you have declared yourself high maintenance from the very beginning?

My husband, Scott, was zero help. His immediate response was, "Yes, we should go!"

Eugene said, "Listen, it's not that bad. I even brought my mother-in-law with me once."

That comforted me until I realized later that I forgot to ask him if he even liked his mother-in-law.

"Don't worry! When we get there, if anything goes wrong and should we get separated, I will show you, by looking at the sun's direction, how to know where Turkey is. And all you have to do is head that way."

How is this seriously even a real conversation? No! I asked my final question to gauge how safe it was: "Would you let your wife go?"

He instantly said, "No." But then he elaborated, "Oh, not because it is dangerous, just because I am old-fashioned."

"If by old-fashioned you mean you have something against your wife being kidnapped and murdered . . ." I turned to my husband. "Honey, tell him you're old-fashioned too! As a matter of fact, I've decided I, too, am old-fashioned!"

Didn't they realize they were talking to someone who had severe panic attacks when flying in an airplane? I did not enjoy being thrown up into the sky in a metal tube. The bravest traveling I had done up to this point was to take a seven-day cruise ship to Mexico on my honeymoon. I don't know if you realize it or not, but they don't just let you go home at will on those things. You are stuck there with endless buffets, massages, and room service for a whole seven days. I don't mean to brag, but with the help of anxiety flashcards (you are OK; you are safe) and buffets, I survived it.

God would not ask me to do such a thing as go to Iraq and be only twenty miles from ISIS.

Once I found out how much it would cost to fly the both of us, I thought surely my financially responsible husband would not want to deplete our savings that much. It seemed a bit wasteful to spend this amount just so we could go for less than a week. Wouldn't that amount of money be better spent donating to poor people? I think I even remember someone saying that very thing in the Bible about what a waste, that it would have been better spent on the poor . . . Wait, it was Judas who said that. Probably don't want to use him as a source for "good ideas."

When I brought it up to Scott, he replied, "I know, I just believe we are supposed to go, so let's not worry about the money."

Not worry about the money? Whatever.

Don't get me wrong here. I love Jesus. I truly believe that Christ is worth dying for and pray the Lord gives me the strength to not waiver in my faith should I ever be put in that position.

Here's the problem. I had actually compiled a list of acceptable ways to die. ISIS in Iraq was not on my approved list. As strange as this may sound, I had even included decapitation on there! I may have an unfair advantage on that one. I get so many migraine headaches that I sometimes get excited about my new heavenly head waiting for me. I can't really claim bravery on that one. So you see, I thought I had been more than generous with the Lord. I thought he should keep life within *my* boundaries.

I couldn't get my husband or Eugene to understand that the Lord would not ask me to face this fear I have of traveling, much less to a war zone. The airport we would be flying into had just shut down for the day because Russia was launching missiles into Syria. If that wasn't bad enough, Turkey was starting to bomb parts of Northern Iraq.

I was forced to move on to those I could count on—my children. I thought surely they would be the voice of reason. I decided to talk with my daughter because my boys were already over eighteen years old, so it was hard to use them as an excuse, but my daughter was only a sophomore in high school. Of course, she would want me to wait until she graduated. That way I wouldn't be telling the Lord *no*, just *later* (the Christian way of telling God no).

My daughter's response was, "Mom, if you have a chance to go to Iraq to encourage those girls, you should totally go. After all, Mom, I'll be eighteen in two years. I'll be fine. If something happens, we will see you again in heaven. Hey, wait, does that mean my brother will be in charge of me? Can't I be in charge of myself?"

"Why do I even keep you around? Thanks for nothing."

Next, my attention turned to my best friend. My Gina. I just knew she would speak some reason into this situation. I talked to her about it as I was walking into Bible study. I ended with, "Can you believe my family?" She was my last hope, but her only concern was whether she would be able to go too.

I really didn't think she was serious, but she called me back that afternoon, asking when we were leaving. I didn't know if the organization would let her. It's not like an open invitation to the public. But I'd ask.

Gina had many hurdles to overcome. First, the organization had to approve of her going. Check! Her husband had to say yes. Check! She had to raise $3,000 in a few weeks' time. Screeching brakes! My friend Gina is rich in the Lord and love but poor in finances. That hurdle seemed insurmountable.

During this time, I was struggling with fear of such magnitude, the likes of which I hadn't experienced since facing giants years earlier in my marriage. Fear was truly starting to take over every minute of every day. The ministry group was to travel right after Christmas. They were going to make all the arrangements, book the flights, pay for them, and then we would reimburse them. If this was going to be my last Christmas with my children, I wanted to be able to enjoy it without picturing myself kidnapped or dead by the following year. So I was happy to tell the ministry not to book the tickets until Gina could get the money.

I don't know if you have ever struggled with anxiety before, but the way I stop being anxious over something is to play out all worst-case scenarios and then conclude that God will be with me and get me through whatever it is I need to get through. After that process, I no longer fear the (insert whatever event my mind can conjure anxiety about). My mind was coming up with a lot of *really bad* worst-case scenarios that could go wrong with this trip. I was having a hard time making peace with all the scary scenes going on in my head.

I shared with my husband a "Gideon's fleece"[1] I put before the Lord. Just as Gideon in the Bible asked for a sign from God, I would take it as a sign that we were supposed to go on this trip if God provided for Gina financially. Not only was she broke, all her friends were too. With such a short timeline, if God did that, I wouldn't be scared, and I'd know he *was* with us.

Gina had been with me through other life crises, and I wanted her with me on this one too. She was the one who talked with me in the middle of the night when anxiety seemed to overtake my very sanity. I figured if I was going to get kidnapped by ISIS, then I wanted my best girlfriend with me. I told Scott it was going to take a miracle for Gina to get financed for this trip.

The next day during my prayer time, I prayed, "Lord, please provide for Gina. This would be such a burden on her family. I don't even know who to ask to help sponsor her." The very second I finished the sentence, I received a text from a girl from Bible study I didn't know very well and who knew nothing about my trip. It read, "Hi Anna, this is so-and-so. I felt like the Lord wanted me to tell you that I have money and I have time, so if you have a need, do not hesitate to ask me."

What in the world? No way!

"That is not what she meant, Lord. She knows I work with refugees. It's right before Christmas, and she probably means she has an extra $20 and wants to buy a few Christmas presents or something. She does not mean $3,000 so Gina can get to Iraq." I was almost too embarrassed to call her and say, "As a matter of fact, I do need money—just a spare $3,000." But I did.

"Hey, so-and-so, this is Anna. I just called to tell you that the timing of your text is really strange. I was just sitting in my recliner, doing my daily prayer time, and the second I finished saying, 'Lord I don't even know who to ask to help sponsor Gina for $3,000,' I got your text. Please know that I'm sure this is not what you meant at all, so no pressure. I'm not even asking you. Just wanted to call and tell you, wow, that's strange timing."

She responded, "Anna, let me tell you something. I own a small business, and I have saved every dollar I have made this year. I have $30,000 saved up in my bank account, and I just prayed and asked the Lord who would he like me to tithe my $3,000 to. So, I would like to write your friend a check for $3,000."

Even with my fleece, I was still scared, and I still couldn't get God to shut a door no matter what I tried. Not my husband, not my children, not my friend, not even Prayer Warrior Woman Pam at our church. When I told her God may be asking me to make a trip to Iraq, I requested, "Would you please pray that God would shut the door if it is not of him?"

She told me no.

"I think you are praying that enough for both of us, but I will pray for the time God has you there to be used for his glory." Apparently, I was going to have to find an out on my own.

I went back to the Lord. I reminded the Lord that he had asked the wrong girl. "I am not brave! And I have an extremely low pain tolerance. For goodness' sake, Lord, need I remind you I took Vicodin when I got my teeth whitened years ago? I have such terrible migraines. I don't have the health for this. *I'm way too weak for what You're asking me to do.*"

Yet in my trepidation, he encouraged me. God always uses the daily passages from my One-Year Bible to speak to me. I don't know how he does it. That morning's reading said:

This is the message from the one who is holy and true, the one who has the key of David. What he opens, no one can close; and what he closes, no one can open. "I know all the things you do, and I have opened a door for you that no one can close. You have little strength, yet you obeyed my word and did not deny me." (Revelation 3:7–8)

It was as if God were speaking directly to me.

The Lord knew just how much encouraging I needed. The next Sunday's church service seemed to be written just for me. Even my husband was laughing throughout the service at how the message spoke to my situation. He was laughing and smiling while his brave warrior of

Christ was literally sobbing and ugly crying in the back row of the small church. I clearly remember the Lord saying to me, "Will you be obedient even when it doesn't make any sense?" Through buckets of snot and tears, I said, "Yes, Lord, I will."

I was a broken mess driving home from that service. I told the Lord, "If that is what you want from me, I will go. But I *really* need you to help me with all this fear." I had finally made peace with *I'm not getting out of this*. This was the road the Lord had called me to. So once again, I prayed a prayer similar to the one I had prayed many years ago after an emotional breakdown. I had been overwhelmed with the realization that it was official: My husband no longer loved me nor cared even the slightest for my well-being (so very different from the changed man who took me to Iraq). I prayed, "Lord, if you aren't going to deliver me from these circumstances, then please make me strong in the midst of them. Show me how to have peace even when my circumstances are not peaceful."

In preparation for my visit to Iraq, I had to go back to the battle plan I had put together all those years ago when my future seemed so uncertain. I had to learn how to find my peace in Christ alone. I was reminded of the first time the Lord asked this of me when the Lord sought to set my husband free of his addictions and anger. The plan didn't make sense to me then either. "If you want to save your marriage, be willing to lose your marriage." Would I be willing to risk everything I loved to be obedient to God, regardless of the cost?

What really landed me on a plane headed to ISIS territory didn't really start with a breakfast conversation with Eugene. It started many years ago when a young woman who had always struggled with fear married a man with anger and sexual addiction issues, and God set them both free.

2

GOING BACK FOR OTHERS

"But this will be your opportunity to tell them about me."

LUKE 21:13

BEFORE I WAS MARRIED, I was an EMT and briefly a paid-call firefighter. Not because I was brave (I am the world's biggest chicken) but because I've just always wanted to help the hurting. I remember once hearing this quote: "Courage is not the absence of fear, but rather the assessment that something else is more important than fear."[1]

That, my sweet friend, is why I am writing. I can't walk by people who are bleeding out when I've been given some experience on what and *Who* can stop the bleeding. Even if it means I will attract the critics and rubberneckers (people who aren't there to offer help but just look).

Sexual addiction is spreading faster than a brush fire with raging winds (can you tell my husband is a retired firefighter?). Just a couple of weeks ago, our not-so-big-city news station, which has time to include what the schools are having for hot lunch each day, told the story about how two girls were forced into the sex trade. The sex trade is a billion-dollar business. Why? Because of demand. Sexual addiction has made its way into every society around the world. No one is immune to its effects.

I meet lots of women who tell me things they wouldn't tell most anyone. Things they are ashamed of or devastated by, things they wish they could shove in a closet, and things they wish they could pretend never happened. They tell me because I know; I've been there. I always tease that I don't have skeletons in the closet because I like to keep mine in the family room where I can keep an eye on them. Pretending you don't have cancer really does not have a good outcome. It just gets progressively worse. Same goes for sexual addiction or any abusive relationship.

I feel it is now time for my commercial interruption, and I must do a disclaimer like you always hear when they are advertising a prescription drug. I am not a professional counselor, nor am I a seminary student. I am just a woman who is oh-so-passionate about her Jesus and how he has guided her through some pretty intense storms. If you currently find yourself in a domestic violence situation, please call your local hotline for support and referrals to counselors who are trained in this area. Marriage counselors are amazing gifts from God, but you need someone who specializes in *these* issues, and not every counselor is experienced in this area.

When discussing how to handle marriage, addiction, and physical and emotional abuse issues in the church, very strong opinions about the godly way to deal with such issues usually come up. I'm going to share with you my journey. I know when I was in the midst of my trials, I desperately wanted a guaranteed, foolproof, five-point plan of how to save my marriage. I never received such a book. Sorry to disappoint you, but this is not one either. This is my story of trusting Jesus to guide me when I didn't know what to do.

I can relate to the story of the blind man in John 9:25b: "But I know this: I was blind, and now I can see!" The religious people of his day were angry at him and wanted to debate religious issues. He was just grateful for what the Lord did for him and didn't want to get into the debate, but rather share what the Lord had done and worship him.

Although I may have many reasons why I *don't* want to tell my story, here is a reason *for* telling my story. I have great news for the hurting, the broken, the prisoner of addiction, or the prisoner of fear. Psalm 96:2–3 says, "Sing to the Lord; praise his name. Each day proclaim the good news that he saves! Publish his glorious deeds among the nations. Tell everyone about the amazing things he does!"

People always ask my husband, "What do you guys do with all that free time you have now that you have retired?" I think I'm going to answer, "We Psalm 96:2–3 all day, every day!" So that is what I am doing and love doing most every day, proclaiming and publishing that Jesus is still in the saving, life-transforming business! And I have to tell you, I get pretty excited when I start talking about the *amazing* things he does.

Come with me! Let me introduce you to my sweet Jesus. He has been waiting for you. God wants you to know "before I formed you in the womb I knew you, before you were born I set you apart." (Jeremiah 1:5, NIV) Even before you were born, the Lord knew everything about you and loved *you*. Although your current situation may have caught you by complete surprise, it most definitely did not catch God by surprise. Oh, there is so much I want to share with you! Let's do coffee together (well, tea for me), but you go grab whatever hot drink brings you joy.

Sometimes I just want to yell like my sweet niece did the night she encountered Jesus for the first time. She had moved in with us while going to college. We were doing a family devotional, and Scott was reading from a book called *Radical* by David Platt. He was reading the Scripture where Jesus said, "If you want to be my disciple, you must, by comparison, hate everyone else—your father and mother, wife and children, brothers and sisters—yes, even your own life. Otherwise, you cannot be my disciple." (Luke 14:26) Not exactly your seeker-friendly Scripture. My niece stood up and basically told us we were all nuts. I told my husband maybe we should have picked something else for our devotion that night. I'm not sure how many days later she left a church service one night, crying and banging her steering wheel, saying over and over again, "God is real! God is real! God is real!" Followed by, "Why am I crying? I don't cry."

It's not about us, *but God!* He can turn people's lives around in an instant. This is me writing about things that I have witnessed in my life and want to yell to everyone: God is real! God is real!

3

———————————

IS PORN A BIG DEAL?

"It is as though we have devised a form of heroin 100 times more powerful than before, usable in the privacy of one's own home and injected directly to the brain through the eyes."[1]

DR. JEFFREY SATINOVER OF PRINCETON UNIVERSITY,
DESCRIBING PORN'S EFFECT TO A U.S. SENATE
COMMITTEE

PORN IS BECOMING WIDELY ACCEPTED, even by many Christian leaders, pastors, counselors, and professors. A professor at a Christian university told a man that my husband was mentoring, "Porn isn't real; it's just pixels on a screen." A woman shared with me how one counselor told her that her husband going to a strip club was not a big deal because "they are just props."

I love my Christian brothers fiercely as much as my sisters. I don't think any less of my brothers or sisters who are caught up in this, but we need to start treating porn as heroin. No one says, "They only use heroin occasionally, so it's no big deal."

I have a sweet sister in Christ who is still battling to break free from her porn habit. She has been clean from her cocaine habit for months now but still struggles with porn. I mentioned to her there is a lot of research out there comparing porn to heroin and asked if she concurred. She absolutely agreed. She shared that it was easier to give up her cocaine habit. I am so glad the Lord brought this sweet young girl into my life. It takes a brave soul to be honest with such struggles.

So is porn really that big of a deal? Some proponents of porn say it helps to spice up your marriage. Not only does porn *not* spice up the marriage, but it destroys it.

When a person watches porn, their brain releases a chemical called dopamine. Dopamine is a chemical that makes you feel incredibly awesome (think best chocolate EVER on steroids). At first this doesn't sound or feel like a bad thing, does it? One of the many problems with this is that porn causes the brain to dump more dopamine at one time than the brain is naturally designed to process. Researchers have discovered that the brain fixes this problem by cutting back on dopamine receptors. With less receptors invited to the dopamine brain party, users need even a higher level of dopamine to achieve the same high as before.[2]

How does a person get the same high? They need to watch harder, more shocking material to overcome their tolerance of what they were originally viewing. Many users discover they must combine sexual material with violent material to achieve the same release. That is why so much porn is filled with images of women being harmed or humiliated. Before you know it, something that once disgusted you begins to turn you on sexually.

Yesterday, I had the privilege of listening to one of Father God's sweet precious daughters share her story with me. She was sexually abused from a very young age. That trauma led to her trying to medicate her pain with feeling loved any way she could. Her boyfriend introduced her to drugs, followed by introducing her to a pimp. She became an online prostitute. She shared how one man asked her to put a dog collar on him and walk him around and even force him to eat dog food. I am usually focused on the abuse of women. But yesterday my heart broke not only for this beautiful young girl sitting before me but for all the sons of my sweet heavenly Daddy who wants to break them free of such demonic bondage.

What happened in that man's life? I wondered. You usually don't wake up one day out of the blue wanting someone to humiliate you so you can be turned on sexually or be fed dog food. It is progressive by needing something new and shocking to watch and possibly act out. This reminds me of a Bible passage describing the lure of an adulterous woman that results in death:

> She calls out to men going by who are minding their own
> business. "Come in with me," she urges the simple. To those who
> lack good judgment, she says, "Stolen water is refreshing; food
> eaten in secret tastes the best!" But little do they know that the
> dead are there. Her guests are in the depths of the grave.
> (Proverbs 9:15–18)

The more one watches, the more one will crave it, and the deeper the pathways become in the brain. The cycle becomes next to impossible to break. Thankfully, we serve a God who specializes in impossible situations. (see Luke 8:27)

I was conflicted about adding the disclaimer, "If you are squeamish, look away." Sometimes when I talk with Christian ladies, they don't want to hear about such topics. Yet we all need to know how to speak to our children, so we can prepare them for how to live in a pornified world. Because if you live where there is internet and your children are presumably not locked in a basement with no access to other human beings with cell phones, your kids are at risk.

Christians are not immune to the draw of porn. I have talked with Christian wives whose "Christian" husbands have secretly recorded them, asked them to get naked in the passenger seat of a car, and "play with themselves" while driving so people can watch. Not knowing this information helps nobody.

I've heard a lot over the years while meeting with women, but this article by Melinda Tankard Reist was especially heartbreaking.

Columnist Allison Pearson was having dinner out with her

girlfriends. One of the women happened to be a general practitioner and goes by the name of Sue in Allison's article. The conversation shifted to how to raise balanced kids in a pornified world and how things are much worse than people suspect. There have been a growing number of teenage girls with internal injuries due to pressure from peer boys to have anal sex despite the excruciating pain and injuries the girls had to endure. These had been underage girls from middle-class, loving, and stable homes.[3]

Melinda Tankard Reist is also hearing from medical professionals that

> young girls (many under-age) are increasingly suffering anal tearing as a result of porn-inspired anal sex acts, including group acts. Some end up with rectums so damaged they are rendered incontinent and need colostomy bags. Other girls are contracting the HPV virus through oral sex. Some end up requiring surgery for throat cancer as a result. Girls have a right to know this is how they could end up. But where do they go for this information? It's hardly mainstream. And online porn presents these acts as standard. Girls who don't want to submit to anal sex start to think there is something wrong with them. One of their biggest fears is being labelled a prude, or "hung up."[4]

And that is what made me cry. I have sat across from women who tearfully shared similar things with me. I know this is a reality because I've experienced the pressure to accept things I did not want to do. But to have young, sweet innocent girls dealing with it . . . young teenage girls needing colostomy bags and surgery for throat cancer from oral sex . . . it's just all too much for this momma to handle.

After reading this article, I prayed that God would make a way for me to have this conversation with my daughter. I take God at his word when he says that we can and should take *all* of our concerns to him, I believe he meant all! (See 1 Peter 5:7.) Even how to start a conversation with your children about anal sex. I've had moms tell me that it would be too embarrassing. Embarrassment I can handle. Having my daughter come to me after the fact, needing a colostomy bag because I was scared of having an embarrassing conversation, that I cannot handle. God created sex. Don't let the world or Satan lead the conversation about it.

I thought I was ahead of the game when my daughter was only fifteen. Apparently not. She told me she had heard of anal sex in junior high because there was a video going around showing it. She had never seen it but had heard many people talking about it. Some girls didn't consider it as having sex because they couldn't get pregnant from it.

What are we teaching our girls? We are teaching them in our homes how a woman should be treated. What are our girls learning when they see women—Jesus-loving women—reading books like *50 Shades of Gray*, where it is considered exciting to have a man inflict pain? I know I'm meddling here, and I'm probably going to get the judgmental, prude card thrown my way, but we were meant for so much more.

I will never forget the look on a young mother's face as she sat across the table at a restaurant, fighting back tears and asking me, "Is it OK to say no?" And sharing how bad it hurt, but her husband always pressured her and got angry when she told him no. I will *never* forget the look of relief on her face when I told her she absolutely did not have to submit to that. No one ever tells girls it is alright to refuse submitting to such requests.

Our Father in heaven must weep over the injury his daughters are submitting to. Many of us submit to such things because we fear man's rejection, and other women submit because they, too, have had their minds corrupted because of abuse at a young age or by porn addiction. I'm not trying to shame anyone. I, too, had to renew my mind from the years of not protecting my mind, because in the beginning of our relationship, I cared more about pleasing my spouse than the Lord. As a result, I found the things I desired changed and were far from God's plan. As Lee Grady puts it in his book *Ten Lies the Church Tells Women*, "A Christian woman's identity is to be found in Christ alone. He makes her complete, whether she has a husband and twelve children or if she remains single all her life. Christ is her life; she is betrothed to Him."[5]

Sex was meant to be beautiful, passionate, bonding, and satisfying for *both* people—not meant to include colostomy bags at the end of it. I know I'm on a soapbox now (I've actually never seen anyone stand on a soapbox before. I gotta say I kind of want to.) But this does get me emotional. The thought of young girls, old girls, and in between girls being so desperate for love that no price is too high for them to pay breaks my heart.

I have listened to young married women as they told horror stories of what their husband was asking them to do. The list is long and dark. As I was talking with a young wife and mother, encouraging her to put up healthy boundaries, her husband was texting her all the submit-to-your-husband Scriptures. She was sobbing about the physical pain and humiliation from the things her husband would ask her to do. I encouraged her to communicate with him that the next time he asked such things of her to say, "I love you and love being with you, but what's even more important than my love for you is I am a daughter of the Most High King, and my body is HIS temple, not mine. I can no longer allow you to abuse his temple." If he didn't agree to treat God's temple with dignity, she should just walk out of the room. I also encouraged this woman to not return home unless her husband agreed to seek help. They needed the support of a professional counselor.

She stayed with us for a few days. It was difficult to convince her to remain until her husband got help. He finally agreed to get help if she would just come home. She did. As far as I know, he went to one appointment and then things returned to the same. It was sad. I was grateful to lend an ear and reassure her she was not crazy to want her husband to be a godly protector instead of behaving like a predator. She is such a beautiful young woman, if only she could realize it. I pray that the Lord has brought other women into her life to mentor her.

So, is porn a big deal? Jesus thought so. "But I say, anyone who even looks at a woman with lust has already committed adultery with her in his heart." (Matthew 5:28)

God isn't just concerned with actions but also what goes on inside a person. I have always seen this Scripture as focused on the person who was lusting and how serious God takes purity of the mind. Recently, I have seen it in a whole new light of just how much God loves his daughters. I heard Dr. Ted Roberts of Pure Desire ministries share with men: "God isn't just your Father but your Father-in-law. Be careful how you treat his daughters."[6]

Lately, when I have read Matthew 5:28, I have felt so loved and cherished by my Father in heaven. It now shouts love and value to me. Husbands were designed to be our *protectors*, not predators. We are to be precious in a husband's sight, not his prey. A mind on porn reverses God's design and turns the protector into a predator looking for his next prey. We are never meant to be used as sex toys. Our beauty is to be admired and cherished by a committed husband, and more importantly, our Heavenly Dad. He created and formed us. Our bodies are a temple of the Holy Spirit and were designed to be wonderfully sexual to our loving husbands. Our Savior values women. Jesus, our Savior, values you!

Not only am I in awe of and grateful for Christ's love for me and my sisters but also for my brothers in Christ. This Scripture just continues to grow richer in meaning the more I research this topic. Jesus also had his sons' best interest at heart as well. Research is catching up with Jesus.

At an American Urological Association's annual meeting in Boston, it was discussed how porn-addicted men are more likely to suffer from erectile dysfunction and be less satisfied with sexual intercourse.[7] Thankfully, the experts have good news to share. According to research, men's sexual performance will return to a baseline if they step away from viewing porn for a few months. Even those who are considered porn addicts will "tend to experience a sexual rejuvenation when they step away from pornography, though this revival make [sic] take a bit longer to manifest."[8]

One therapist had this to share at the annual meeting.

This is hardly a surprise to therapists such as myself who specialize in sex and intimacy issues, including the compulsive use of pornography. Porn addicted clients have been telling us, ever since the early days of the internet, things like:

- My girlfriend says it feels like I'm "not there" when we're having sex. And she complains that it takes me way too long to reach orgasm.

- I get super hard when I'm looking at porn, but when I'm with a real woman I struggle to both get and maintain an erection.
- When I'm having sex with my wife, I'm thinking about porn. Otherwise, I just can't get it up. I think I might prefer porn sex to real sex.[9]

Oh, how I wish I would've known this in our early years of marriage. I remember being at a women's Bible study at a mentor's house, crying because my husband was never interested in having sex with me. I liked having sex with him and thought about it often. I shared with them the only way he ever seemed interested was if we were watching porn.

I think of a young girl who was a preacher's kid and homeschooled. Once she was married, she couldn't understand why her husband (who was in seminary school at the time) didn't want to have sex with her. She would ask, "Is something wrong with my genitals? Maybe they aren't normal" (because that is what her husband told her). Only to find out later he was a regular visitor to strip bars and a variety of online sex culture. There was nothing wrong with how God created her womanhood; her husband had corrupted his mind.

> Your eye is like a lamp that provides light for your body. When your eye is healthy, your whole body is filled with light. But when it is unhealthy, your body is filled with darkness. **Make sure that the light you think you have is not actually darkness.** If you are filled with light, with no dark corners, then your whole life will be radiant, as though a floodlight were filling you with light. (Luke 11:34–36, emphasis mine)

I think this passage relates to how people think porn is going to improve their sex life but ends up destroying it. This seems to scream, "Don't fall for it! It is nothing but darkness!"

Have you ever heard the argument that porn is between consenting adults, and it doesn't hurt anyone? That is a lie. But an addicted spouse will often use this justification to make the other feel like they're making a big deal out of nothing.

Porn contributes to sex trafficking. There are countless stories of women thinking they signed up for one thing, for example, modeling or other type of employment, but ended up getting a completely different experience of drugging, rape, and beatings, all while being filmed. I have friends who work with victims of sex trafficking. When you hear their stories, consent is hardly the word I would use to describe it. I started to research what porn stars themselves thought about it, and frankly it hurt my heart too much to continue. It is such a dark industry. I will only share this one quote from a former porn star.

According to Regan Starr, a former porn actor, "I got the &*%$ kicked out of me. . . . Most of the girls start crying because they're hurting so bad. . . . I couldn't breathe. I was being hit and choked. I was really upset and they didn't stop. They kept filming. [I asked them to turn the camera off] and they kept going."[10]

As former NFL player and actor Terry Crews put it: "It changes the way you think about people. People become objects. People become body parts; they become things to be used rather than people to be loved."[11]

Well, that is a lot of depressing information to digest. But before I risk losing you, let me encourage you, don't quit!

This story you are about to read has a good ending, and so will yours, regardless of what happens to your marriage. I can say that because a beautiful marriage or a not-so-beautiful marriage is temporary. I get to share with you something that is eternally beautiful: the never-ending love of Jesus. That, my friend, is worth reading on.

4

GROWING UP

<blockquote>

"Growing up is such a barbarous business, full of inconvenience and pimples."[1]

J. M. BARRIE, AUTHOR OF *PETER PAN*

</blockquote>

I GREW up in a small town that basically felt like Mayberry to me. I was quite the tomboy. I loved playing sports. Pretty high energy. And from what I've been told, I would say whatever popped into my head. Unlike now, there was no editor to come behind me and filter my words. As far as school went . . . let's just say, I wasn't always the teacher's favorite. Even though I had a speech problem growing up that sent me to *many* years of speech therapy, I talked a lot. Still do, except now I can pronounce my R's—most of the time.

I always seemed to struggle with fear and anxiety, although I had never heard anyone call it that while I was growing up. All I knew was that sometimes I would get these feelings like something was wrong with me and I was going to die. These feelings would come up unexpectedly. I remember my first day of high school like it was yesterday. Apparently, so did a few people from my twenty-year high school reunion.

I was so nervous because I was coming from a private Catholic school and going into a public high school. I went from eight years of plaid skirts and navy-blue knee-highs to you could wear whatever you want. (I always like to blame my lack of fashion sense due to forced uniforms during my formative years.) I remember arriving at what felt like a huge college campus, but wasn't, and seeing a group of girls standing in a circle I knew from playing city sports. I thought, *No problem. I can fit in. I will just go stand right next to them.* And then I started to feel my fruit loops starting to loop.

While I was standing there trying to fit in, horror struck me as I realized my breakfast was trying to break out. I took off running in hopes of finding a restroom before it was too late. But it was not to be. I threw up in the hallway as kids jumped out of the way to avoid the . . . well, some details are better left unsaid. Just know this anxiety thing of mine caused me some high school trauma.

First days of school were not the only thing that would bring on my anxiety attacks. Usually, the other was boys. I would have crushes. (Do they even say crushes anymore? According to my teenage daughter, they refer to boys they like as their "bae"—*before anyone else*.) I liked boys. I liked them a lot growing up, right until they liked me back, and then I wanted to throw up.

During my freshman year, I was asked to the prom. I made it until the first dance when I felt my date do a slight rub on my open-back dress, and you guessed it! Off to the bathroom, with nerve issues followed by an early drive home. It's nice knowing how I probably come up in dinner conversations when kids ask their parents about the worst date they ever went on. Why, that would have been with me!

I could never figure out why dating made me so nervous. I made it through high school with having two boyfriends—one lasted about two weeks and the other about a month. However, all of high school was not a loss for me. It was there that I heard my first motivational speaker. I went to a conference with our high school key club and heard Terry Bradshaw speak. He was so funny and inspiring. It was the first time I heard about a job called "motivational speaker." I was really drawn to such speakers after that event.

My sophomore year, my parents moved me to the high desert, which was way different than Mayberry. It was there that I joined the Future Farmers of America (FFA). It was at a national FFA conference, listening to Zig Ziglar speak, that I felt like I had a call on my life. I can't explain it other than it felt like a spiritual experience. I knew I was supposed to encourage people who didn't know their worth in life. I didn't know what that would look like or how to get there, just that I felt compelled it was what I was created for.

As soon as I graduated from high school, I called a speaker's bureau and asked how someone became a motivational speaker. (This was before the internet was invented and dinosaurs still walked the earth.) The secretary told me about a book that described how to break into the public speaking market. She also recommended I find a local Toastmasters group to work on my public speaking skills. She didn't have any women speakers who could hold a crowd's attention, so if I was any good, she had a gold mine of opportunities waiting for me. I hung up the phone confident I would be that woman.

There were only two things holding me up. One was that most motivational speakers had accomplished something in their lives. I was eighteen, barely graduated from high school with nothing but a desire to encourage people. The second obstacle I wouldn't figure out until I tried public speaking. I discovered that boys liking me weren't the only thing that caused my stomach to turn with fear. Not knowing what to do next, I followed my sister to college.

It was there that I have my first memory of crossing paths with one of those crazy, Jesus-loving, born-again Christians. They sure were a different bunch. They lived differently and seemed happy. One sweet girl came over to my dorm room and tried to tell me about having a relationship with Jesus. I remember brushing her off but also being jealous of how happy she seemed.

Being raised Catholic, as far as I knew it, was like being born a certain race: you don't get to choose it, and you can't change it. You just accept it. I was jealous that she seemed to enjoy her "religion." I had always liked God since I was a little girl; I just never liked church. That was the place of sitting still and being quiet. I wasn't very good at it. I was pretty sure having to sit still and being quiet were against the Geneva Conventions. In fact, I remember my dad asking my mom, "Is it possible to get a D in religion class?" Apparently, it is.

I think I'm the only kid who tried to cheat while in the confessional. How is that possible? Well, let me explain. When you go into a Catholic confessional, you have to say a prayer you are supposed to have memorized. Memory work has never been my strong point, so instead I made a cheat sheet to take in with me. The priest on duty one day was the head priest who was very old and very old school. Everyone was scared of messing up. I, on the other hand, had bragged on how I had a foolproof plan of using a cheat sheet for my prayers. It was a great plan until I forgot that the lights go out when you kneel down. All I could remember from the prayer was "Oh, my God, I am heartily sorry. . . oh boy, am I sorry."

I have wonderful memories of going to Catholic school and church, and I know others who are serving Jesus passionately in the Catholic church. But I knew I was missing something. I was missing the joy and peace that young college girl seemed to have.

My time at college was short-lived. I didn't excel at dorm life for the same reason I had to shut down my Facebook page for a season. I wasn't able to resist the twenty-four-hour people party. Yep, home I went. Not sure what I wanted to do with my life, I went back to waitressing. One day at work, I met a woman whose husband taught an EMT course at the local college. It sounded so interesting. Plus, the thought of speeding through the streets, lights flashing and sirens wailing as we raced to save someone, was exciting, so I signed up. For the first time in my life, I *loved* studying. I loved everything about it. Especially the pictures with bones sticking out and such.

I wanted to accomplish something in life, so I could be taken seriously as a motivational speaker. I decided to join a local Toastmasters group, where I met a woman named Glory. There was something different about her—a joy and peace. Even more impressive was she was about to celebrate her thirtieth wedding anniversary. She and her husband acted like newlyweds. Which I found odd yet enviable. We would go out to lunch together and just talk about life. She would tell me about her relationship with Jesus but never be pushy or put down the faith I grew up with.

I loved spending time with her, especially because I was starting to struggle socially for the first time in my life. Throughout my life I had lived with epilepsy and took medication to control it. During my sophomore year in high school, the doctors changed my medication. I had always been athletic and in decent shape. I grew up with a great metabolism and could eat whatever I wanted. That all changed with the new medication. I started to gain weight, but soccer helped keep it in check.

I thought to myself, *Well, I hear the older you get your metabolism changes, and it slows down. I guess I've reached that time of life.* At age sixteen?

So by eighteen, and no sports, the weight kept coming. I was once full of confidence, and now closing in on nearly two hundred pounds, I was becoming depressed. I'll always remember when a group of my friends and I worked at a stockyard and we slept on the floor at a friend's house. When they thought I was sleeping, they made fat jokes about me.

I didn't know Romans 8:28 at the time—about God working all things for our good—but God was doing just that. Not feeling like I fit in with my "friends" anymore, I spent more time with Glory.

As if my weight issue weren't challenging enough, it was about to get harder. I went for a neurology appointment to evaluate the medication I took for seizures. My doctor looked at me and said, "I think we need to change your medicine. One of the side effects to this prescription is weight gain." Now she tells me!

The rest of the appointment was spent telling her about my first car I had just bought. I was so excited; it was all I could think about. I had been going to these appointments since the first grade, so I didn't take her questions too seriously. She asked if I had been having any staring spells lately. I was still distracted with my news and answered, "Oh, I don't know. I could be, but let me get back to telling you about this car I just bought!"

She told me, "Well, I'm going to have to turn this in to the DMV." And with that, I lost my license due to "lapse of consciousness."

Overweight, new car, new car payments, middle of EMT school, and no driver's license. I had plenty of time to hang out with Glory.

Every two years, I had an EEG test, and it was due soon after losing my license. If I was going to get my license back and ever be able to get hired by an ambulance, I really needed a normal EEG reading, which I had never had. I immediately called Glory and asked her to pray for me. She knew I needed a miracle. She invited me to a Christian women's luncheon. I had no idea what that was, but I agreed to go.

Before we ate, they played worship songs, but all I knew was ladies were singing and some were crying, but everyone was singing about this Jesus. After a little while, I made an excuse to Glory that I had forgotten I had to be somewhere else. I wanted no part of a roomful of crying women. That was just too out there for me. But before Glory let me go, she had ladies pray for me and my EEG test. I believe my quote to Glory was, "I have *never* had a normal EEG test before. It will take a miracle." I had more faith that they would find me brain-dead instead of brain-healed. But God blessed me with my first ever normal EEG—just in time to bring to my DMV hearing.

With a clear EEG, the doctor was willing to take me off all medication. With that change and exercise, I started to drop the weight. I was also able to finish and get my EMT certificate but would have to wait almost a year to get my DMV record to remove the "on probation for lapse of consciousness." I would have to go to a DMV hearing to get that removed. I didn't know it at the time, but I would not go to that hearing alone.

My future husband was about to arrive on the scene.

5

HOW WE MET

> "You must be the one. You don't make me want to throw up."
>
> ANNA LUKE

IN A FEW SHORT MONTHS, my husband and I will have completed twenty-four years of marriage. I feel so accomplished saying that, and it still amazes me that we made it here. Throughout our marriage, I always find myself saying, "I don't deserve this!" I still say this. The difference is that in the earlier years of marriage, I meant it as a plea. How could I have done something so terrible to deserve a husband who treats me like this? Now I say it to mean the opposite. What have I done to deserve such an amazing husband? Now, my husband is one of the most godly men I know, and I trust the Lord that we will make it to the finish line that way. The good news that I've learned over the years is that people may fail us, but the Lord never will. I don't have to live in fear of any future mistakes or trials. Jesus is enough!

Scott and I met at a restaurant. My sister's car was in the shop, and she needed a ride to meet her friends to watch Monday night football. My first memory of Scott is him sitting next to me as he graded my sister's papers for her sixth-grade class. I had initially been talking to a couple people on the other side of me. A few of the guys there were paid-call firefighters (part-time firefighters who are usually hoping to get hired full time with a department). My first words to Scott were, "Are you paid-call too?" He said he was a captain with the fire department. That led to me explaining my aspirations to be hired by an ambulance company, and he ended up inviting me to train with his crew as they practiced their EMT skills the next night.

As soon as we were done training, I sat in the weight room at the firehouse talking with Scott until after midnight. We instantly hit it off and could talk for hours. He would tell me about Jesus and talk as if he knew him. He was different than any other man I had ever met.

From that first night, we were together, separated only by work. I decided to train for the paid-call firefighters academy. We enjoyed working out together every day, trying to get me ready for the academy's agility test, then going to get hot fudge sundaes afterwards. Those were really sweet memories.

One time, when we were running stadium stairs at my old high school, I started to slow down, and Scott grabbed my hand and said, "If you want to be a firefighter, you better get your butt moving." He didn't let go of my hand until we reached the top. That's when I put my hand on his shoulder and told him, "I will be your best friend in the whole world if we don't have to run another flight of stairs!"

Scott obliged and we walked out to our cars. I vividly recall telling him, "I will never get married. The only reason to get married is to have kids, and since I don't like kids, that takes away my need for a man! In fact, one way to get rid of me is to give me a ring."

He told me that day, "You will be married in two years or less." I thought to myself, *This man actually thinks he is going to marry me. He won't, but I think it is strange that it isn't scaring me away.*

My declaration never bothered Scott. He once told me, "Your love is like the ocean." I'm thinking big? beautiful? No. "One minute it's in, and the next minute it's out."

Every morning I thought to myself, *What am I doing? This man is so much older than me. We are just friends.* Then he would be so kind and considerate to me after spending the day with him, I thought, *Hmm, maybe I can see a future together.*

I had never seen many happy marriages, so I really didn't see a need for marrying. It's not like I was dead to the idea of romance and dating—I was just never successful at executing it. Besides, it's hard to feel romantic while fighting the urge to vomit from a nervous stomach!

I'm not really sure at what point we officially started dating. I just remember telling him after a few months together, "You must be the one. You don't make me want to throw up."

He replied, "How romantic." He had no idea.

With Valentine's approaching, I told a girlfriend I thought Scott was going to buy me a gold necklace I had seen and liked. Being a waitress at the time, $60 was a lot of money.

I went all out for him, getting him a balloon, a candy bar, and writing on his bathroom mirror "Happy Valentine's Day" in lipstick. He had given me a key to his house, so my girlfriend and I snuck into his house while he was at work. After dinner, we went back to his house. He seemed really nervous, and I couldn't figure out why. After all, nerves were my native language, not his. He said he had gotten me something. He went and grabbed it and handed me a One Year Bible. *How anticlimactic.*

"Thank you. Just what I never knew I really wanted."

After he gave me the Bible, Scott told me he still had something else to give me but looked a bit scared. I thought that was strange. What could he be so nervous about? He said something along the lines of, "I don't want you to freak out or anything. I got you something, but it's not from me. The Lord told me to get this for you." He then gave me a ring box. Inside was a one-carat solitaire diamond ring. I looked at it and was shocked.

"If this is an engagement ring, I can't accept it."

"In my prayer time, I heard very specifically that I was to buy a one-carat diamond ring. I thought it was crazy, but when I went to look at rings and found the one I should get, the price was the exact amount of a check I got in the mail from the fire department for some back pay they owed me. God even provided the exact amount of money just at the right time. So, it is not an engagement ring. This is just me being obedient to God, and it's a gift from God to you."

When I get nervous, I say goofy things. In true me fashion, I said, "Just curious, did God say anything about a matching set of earrings?" He laughed and said no, and then I accepted the ring.

I have always loved my wedding ring, even in our darkest marriage moments, and how it was given to me because before it was ever a wedding ring representing my husband's love to me, it first was a sign of God's love for me. That night, I received two of my most treasured gifts.

With a ring on my hand we became serious. It wasn't long afterward that we decided to get married. He proposed to me at a Toastmasters meeting during his first speech. I had already been a member for a while, and he started attending with me. It made the newspaper: "Fire Chief Proposes to Firefighter" (even though he was a captain).

I remember thinking, *I am so fortunate to be marrying a man who is so kind and gentle.*

One of Scott's coworkers later told me they used a nickname for him behind his back. They would call him The Wolfman. He was known for his temper, but they told me since he started seeing me, he had changed and was a lot nicer. I was so complimented by that and thought, *Oh, how sweet! I have the power to change someone.*

It was a superficial change.

It took me by surprise the first time I saw Scott's other side that I would later in our marriage nickname "Fred." My husband was a funny, caring, godly man. Fred was scary, and at one time, I became pretty convinced the song "Cold as Ice" by Foreigner was a more accurate wedding song. When Fred was around, it didn't matter how sorry I was for accidentally making him mad or how much I would beg him to just tell me what I did wrong, so I could fix it and be a better wife.

The first time I ever saw Fred was before we were married. I was working at the fire department at the time and had just returned to the station from a training burn. Scott happened to be there when I arrived, and he joked as if he were going to dump me in some water. It is a well-known fact in my family, still to this day, that I seriously hate being in wet clothes. I have zero sense of humor about it. All I could think about was how I didn't want to clean and roll fire hoses in a heavy, wet uniform after an already long and tiring day. I wasn't going down without a fight.

In that skirmish, I accidentally kicked Scott in the nose. I didn't mean to. When I got home, he was there, waiting at my parents' house and had prepared everyone to play along that I had broken his nose. He had placed some medical tape on his nose to make it convincing. We went out to the front porch by ourselves, and he acted very angry with me. I explained I was sorry and started crying because I felt so horrible. He just kept going for what seemed like forever, pretending to be in pain. He continued yelling at me, saying I was an out-of-control maniac at the fire station.

Scott finally told me I didn't really break his nose. He just wanted to teach me a lesson. The more I cried and said I was sorry, he seemed to gain satisfaction from it. I was stunned that he saw how horrible I felt, and he didn't care at all. I told him I had hurt him accidentally but that he intentionally set out to hurt me. He didn't stop with his "joke" until he felt like I had had enough. I didn't understand that kind of response at all.

That incident really disturbed me because, up until that point, I had never had someone plan revenge to try and hurt me. I remember sharing this with an older Christian lady I looked up to. I told her I thought my soon-to-be husband had a dark side to him. She told me, "Oh, every man does." I thought I must have been making too much of it and let go the warning sign of what our future marriage struggles would be, thinking it must have been a fluke, just like the time he kicked me out of his house before we were married.

We were engaged at the time. I had an ex-boyfriend that I had only dated a month or two, and even though Sam was married to a nice girl, he would still hang out at my parents' house. He was in the military and didn't have any family around. I come from a slightly crazy (a loving term because everyone knows normal is boring) but loving family. They (especially my mom) had a soft spot for all strays, animals and people alike. The reason our relationship only lasted about a month was because he had a very loud personality and a bad temper. I remember telling him,

"Temper is a deal breaker for me." (Yeah, I know. Is ironic the correct word for this?)

After we broke up, Sam still came around to visit my parents. I *really* didn't like it. I remember telling my parents before I met Scott, "You know why people break up with each other? So they don't have to see the other person anymore. I'm *still* seeing him. He is always here!" My parents told me they couldn't just tell him not to come over anymore. I understood . . . sort of.

The woman my ex had married was a sweet girl who also didn't have a great family life. So my mom loved on her too. Once they were married, they didn't come over often, but it bothered my soon-to-be husband when they did. I told him my parents didn't turn people away. I've always loved that about them, but yes, this one made for awkward moments. He told me to do him a favor and not tell him when my parents did something for them. I agreed to try, but I hated lying and keeping secrets when it felt like I was being deceitful.

Soon, Beth was expecting a baby. With no one to give her a baby shower, my mom offered. I was happy to help. We purposefully scheduled it on one of my husband's shifts, so I knew he would be at work the whole twenty-four hours. I hated being evasive with him that day, but he asked me not to tell him. As we were getting ready for the best part of any shower (eating cake), all of a sudden, Beth dropped to the ground and started having a seizure. A very long one. We called 911.

Guess who heard the call over the radio for a woman having seizures at my address? Scott knew I had a history of epilepsy, and although my parents' house was not in Scott's first due (his coverage area for his engine), he heard the call come in. He called me very worried. I had to tell him, "I'm fine and don't worry. You know how you told me not to tell you when my parents do something for Sam and Beth? Well, we were giving a baby shower for Beth, and she had a seizure."

What were the chances something like this would happen? I told him, "See? We aren't supposed to keep secrets from each other."

Scott refused to speak to me after that. I couldn't figure out why he was so cold to me. I did what he had told me to do! We went to church together the next day, and while driving back to his house, I kept thinking, *How can I get him to understand that my parents love him? They just can't help being kind to others in need.* I couldn't put it into words. Then I remembered reading about the story of the workers in the vineyard in the new pink Bible he had given me.

Jesus shared a parable in Matthew 20:1–16 where, at least in my new understanding of Jesus, he was telling us don't be jealous just because of someone's generosity.

I asked him, "Have my parents ever been unkind or unwelcoming to you? Then please don't be jealous just because they are also kind to others." I thought, *He respects the Bible. We should be good to go.* (I had already started to move some of my things over to his place, excited for our almost wedding date.)

Scott continued to be quiet. When we arrived, I was completely shocked and surprised when he started throwing some of my things at me and yelling, "Get the f— out of my house!"

I was like a deer in headlights for a moment. Then I panicked and thought, *Okay!* I didn't really know what to do, so I picked up the couple things he threw at me and turned to leave. As soon as I did, he ran over and apologized. Everything lasted less than a minute. I remember thinking, *He didn't mean it. Anyone can make mistakes. Right? Besides, he said he was sorry, so we are good. It won't happen again.*

I can't help but picture my younger, barely twenty self and sigh. Poor, naive girl. Those weren't just once-in-a-lifetime appearances by Fred. I had no idea at the time, but Fred would be moving in with us and affecting our marriage for many years to come.

6

EARLY YEARS OF MARRIAGE

"The only true wisdom is in knowing you know nothing."

SOCRATES

OUR WEDDING WAS SUCH A WONDERFULLY exhausting day. I remember laughing my way down the aisle because my dress was too long. Before that moment, I would stand in front of the mirror and lift the front to walk, not thinking when the moment arrived, I would hold my dad's arm with one hand and carry a bouquet of flowers in the other. People were giving me walking tips as I passed them down the aisle. Most of the day was a blur. I just remember a lot of laughter.

Although I had always hoped to save sex until marriage, I fell short of that goal (not blaming Scott for that). I lowered my guard. I had never felt like that for anyone before. But once that door was opened, I was the only one interested in closing it. The times I did try, he would become angry with me, so I would give in. Somehow, the earlier self-confident, I-don't-need-any-man, I'm-fine-by-myself woman was hooked!

The thought of Scott being mad at me made me feel so anxious. When he loved me, I felt so cared for, protected, and most importantly, peaceful. For someone who struggled with anxiety her whole life, peace meant everything to me. I couldn't imagine my life without him.

We went to the mountains for the first night of our honeymoon. In true me fashion, I kicked off that night like most other big events of my life. I threw up. The road was very winding. Halfway there, a quick pullover was needed. Thankfully, my stomach had settled by the time we got to the hotel. The room was beautiful.

Yet it didn't take us long to go further off course in having a God-honoring sex life. They had porn on TV. Our first night together as man and wife included others.

The next day, we headed to a seven-day cruise to Mexico. From the moment we left the altar at the church, it seemed I was no longer "enough." Just being alone was not enough. If not playing a physical movie, he wanted to play a verbal movie in our mind's eye. It seemed like each time, it would have to be something new.

I did not like the scenarios but would rationalize them. What was the harm? It didn't matter what we thought about, as long as it made him happy. He would seem so much more in love with me after these compromises. Trouble was, the imaginary line always seemed to move. And like a drug addict, the "you are the best" love high for him was always temporary.

At times, it seemed he would become convicted about our sex life and stopped pressuring to participate in ungodly sex for a while, but that would turn into no sex life altogether. I remember being newly married, crying at a Bible study, asking the ladies, "What is wrong with me? Why doesn't my husband ever want to be with me?" When I asked Scott about it, he told me, "Sex is overrated." Which translated, "Sex with *me* is overrated."

I had saved myself for my husband. Even though we were intimate before marriage, I knew we were supposed to be together and committed myself to him. I liked sex, a lot, when it could be just us. I shared with the ladies that it seemed like the only time my husband ever wanted to have sex with me was if I would call and tell him to stop by the video store to bring a movie home.

Is porn really such a big deal after all? I was raised not to think it was. "That's just boys being boys."

Outside of our sex life, our first year couldn't have gone better. I have great memories. I got to spend almost every day with my best friend. Then "Fred" came for a visit. I can remember the day because it happened on my birthday. We had arranged to meet my family and some friends at a restaurant. Before our dinner arrangements, my husband was going to have his first hockey game of the season. We went to the arena to wait for his game to start. Unfortunately, they were running over two hours behind schedule. Those waiting for us had paid for childcare.

The other guys on the team heard it was my birthday and our plans to celebrate. They told my husband they had plenty of guys to play and not to worry about it—go enjoy dinner. My husband, on the other hand, didn't want to miss his game. He finally agreed but was mad that I wanted him to choose my birthday. He didn't speak to me on the ride home. When we arrived, I told him, "You are joking, right? You are not really mad about having to miss one game because of my birthday dinner?" He wasn't joking. Our friends came over to pick us up, and he wouldn't get in the car. I went by myself with our friends. It was an awkward night.

I tried to speak with him the next morning, but I was taken by surprise once again. He started throwing objects at me, calling me all sorts of names, and yelling at the top of his lungs, "Get the f— out of my house!"

I was so scared. I can remember it like it was yesterday. I ran out of the house with nothing. I didn't know where to go. Too embarrassed to go to a neighbor's house, I just kept crying and walking, not sure where I should go to call my parents (this was before cell phones). I remembered my husband's boss lived a few streets over, and I had made friends with his wife, Karen. They were believers and very nice, so I decided I would go there.

Thankfully, she was home.

Karen drove me to my parents' house. The next day, she had her teenage sons help me move while Scott was at work. Her husband made sure Scott stayed at the station while we were moving my stuff out. The station wasn't far from our house, so Scott would stop by sometimes with the crew to say hi or grab a snack. I was scared he might do that while I was moving out, so I was extremely grateful to have them help me make sure that didn't happen.

So there I was, shortly after being married, thrown out of "his" house over a hockey game. I thought surely, after a day, he would settle down and realize how foolish this was and call for me to return. I left him a letter on the table. I can't remember everything I said in the letter, but I remember telling him how I was foolish enough to overlook the first time this happened when we were dating.

Right before we got married, I had called off the wedding because I had told Scott I wanted to work on an ambulance for our first year of marriage. He wanted a wife who would stay home with future kids. My mom was a stay-at-home mom and I loved that, so I gave my word I would work for a year then quit for us to have kids and be at home with them. He refused to agree, so I told him if he couldn't compromise, I would not marry him. He called two days later and said he didn't want to lose me. I could work a year if I wanted to.

In my letter to him, I referenced that incident. I shared I was in agreement to be a future stay-at-home mom, but not if he was going to use money as power over me. I also told him I had forgiven him when he kicked me out of his house when we were dating. But here we were married, and he still referred to it as his house, so he could kick me out at his whim. I foolishly assumed it would be different once we were married. I would not make the mistake of assuming this wouldn't happen once we had children together.

I honestly thought, *Surely he loves me and will call me to apologize and work things out.* A week went by with no phone call. Then two. I was having such anxiety. I couldn't take it any longer and called our pastor and asked him to go over to the house to talk with him.

The pastor called me and asked me to come back home and talk. During that talk, we agreed that Scott should see a counselor for his anger. I remember driving with him to his counselor's appointment and sitting in the waiting room while he went in by himself. He came out looking happy. On the way home, he shared with me what the counselor told him he should tell me. It went something like this: "I have a really stressful job, and it is important for me to have a hobby to help relieve that stress, so you need to be more understanding and let me play hockey."

I was shocked. What in the world did he tell that woman in there? I supported him playing hockey. I loved watching him play hockey. I just asked him to miss one game, so people weren't waiting for us for *my* birthday party. That was his only counseling appointment for his temper until a few years later.

That fight had a *huge* effect on me. It made me realize that as far as my husband was concerned, I was disposable to him. Most of the time he would be so loving, the best husband, kind and caring. But it put a fear in me that I could be disposed of at a moment's notice over something as simple as, well, a hockey game. It left me insecure in our relationship and scared to make him mad.

Shortly after that, I became pregnant with our first son. Also, around this time, we had new neighbors move in across the street from us, Pat and Steve. They were an older Christian couple. Spending time with Pat was like spending time with Jesus himself. She was so kind and loving. If you ever tried to compliment her, she would always say, "I don't know about that. I just know the Lord is good." I loved to go visit her in the evenings when my husband was at work and I was pregnant and lonely.

Once my son was born, it was harder to go visit Pat at night. I would look across the street and see the light on in her family room, knowing she was sitting in her chair every night, reading her Bible. One night, I decided to pick up the One Year Bible[1] my husband had given me when we were dating and started reading it. For the first time in my life, the Bible was coming alive for me.

It was around this time the internet was making its way into people's homes. I know it will be hard for some of you to imagine, but there was no social media at this time except for a thing called "chat rooms." No webcams or pictures, just people with fake screen names.

Shortly after I married Scott, I went to a Zig Ziglar conference and bought his series called *Courtship after Marriage*. Scott and I agreed to live by the standards he presented about never being alone with the opposite sex and not having private, personal relationships with the opposite sex. We agreed that fidelity and protecting our marriage was one of the greatest gifts we could give our children. Zig Ziglar talked about how he would never even get in a car alone with another woman when he traveled for speaking events. He made sure if a woman picked him up at the airport that there were two. *Never alone with the opposite sex.* We both agreed and shared with others the wisdom of choosing to live that way. I tried to make sure I never held private conversations with the opposite sex.

With that in mind, I joined a Christian women-only chat room for a short while. It was here that I picked the name for our second son because one woman had her son's name as her screen name. I think that every other pregnant woman must have been in the same chat room because when I first took our second son to church nursery, there were three other boys with the same name.

I remember telling my husband about some of the things we talked about in the chat rooms and joking how I could be talking about baby things with some creepy guy and not even know it. Scott said he thought chat rooms were a waste of time and it wasn't wise to hang out talking to strangers. I will always remember feeling so blessed that I was married to such a godly husband who valued me. Especially since one of my friends had discovered a huge phone bill from her husband calling 900 phone numbers.[2] I felt so fortunate that I could trust my husband . . . or so I thought.

7

THE TOWERS CAME DOWN

EVER SINCE MY husband was a little boy, he knew he wanted to be a fireman. His mom would share stories of him as a little boy playing with toy fire trucks. Funny thing was, he never grew out of that. When I married him, he had a case of collectable fire trucks that were his babies. He kept some of them in a display case so people and kids could look at but, of course, not touch. Being a fireman was so much of who he was. It was "in his blood," as they say.

From my perspective, despite the trials, life had been mostly good. Scott and I were best friends and did everything together. Sure, there was the hockey fight where he threw me out of the house, but my husband was a great husband.

Thankfully, Fred usually only showed up once or twice a year in the early years of our marriage, and the rest of the time was awesome. But ever since the hockey fight in our first year, I was always aware of Fred's existence and was always afraid of activating him. It kind of reminded me of being married to the Hulk, just with a few less muscles and not so green. I worked hard to not make him mad.

My husband valued me, but Fred thought I was disposable. I was always trying to make sure I did things his way so he could be happy. I learned that I could only be happy if he was happy with me. (I need a nap just thinking about how much work that was to take on the responsibility for someone else's happiness.)

Fred was mean and unforgiving if he felt you wronged him (which didn't take much). He would break things or just throw things that I valued in the trash—things that were precious to me. My mother-in-law once shared with me that her husband used to throw her things out when he would get mad at her too. I asked my husband about that years ago, and he never knew his dad used to do that. I found it interesting how that certain generational curse had carried on, albeit unwittingly.

Closing in on our sixth anniversary, we started having a few more Fred moments. During one of my quiet times, I felt like the Lord wanted me to write down all the things I loved about my husband. After writing them down, I decided to frame it and give it to him as an anniversary present.

This is what I framed:

I love that you came home in your turnouts[1] carrying flowers for me.
I love that you make siren noises and jump up and down on the engine when the kids sit on the fire engine.
I love that you are such a great father and you adore your children.
I love that you do a Chippendales dance that is more funny than sexy, especially at weddings!
I love that you held me while I was in labor for our daughter and read Scriptures to me.
I love that you cried when our oldest was born.
I love that the day I found out when I was pregnant with our first child and that I needed to get a breast biopsy because the doctors thought I might have breast cancer like my mom had at an early age, you wept because you were scared you were going to lose me.
I love that when I was having a rough time after having our first child and the doctors referred me to the psych department for

postpartum depression, you encouraged me the whole time that it
was normal and I had nothing to be embarrassed about.
I love that I have woken you up in the middle of the night because
I was scared, and I wanted you to pray for me or the kids. You
always do without a complaint.
I love that you can fix anything and that you are so smart.
I love that when we get separated in the store, I can always find
you in the toy section, even if you don't have the kids with you.
I love that you never refer to our money as "your money" just
because you are the only one who brings in a paycheck.
I love that you are faithful at giving money back to God.
I love that you are not financially impulsive.
I love that you hold my hand in the car.
I love that you always compliment me on being a good mother to
other people.
To put it simply, I love you for being you. You are a wonderful,
godly man, husband, and father. We complete each other.
Happy 6th anniversary

And he really was all those things. That was the space we lived in a lot of the time. I believe, looking back, that God had me write that not for my husband but for me, because things were about to get ugly in our house. Fred was going from an occasional, unwanted guest who would stop by unannounced to being a permanent resident. I needed something tangible to hold on to, something to help me see through the rubble of our marriage crash, something to remind me what I would be fighting for.

The year leading up to 9/11, I was changing because of God's Word. I did not grow up reading the Bible. I went to church each week and heard portions read but never read it in its entirety. It's not like anyone kept me from it; it just was never on my radar. So for the first time I read the Scripture, "Do you not know that your bodies are temples of the Holy Spirit, who is in you, whom you have received from God? You are not your own." (1 Corinthians 6:19) That was life transforming stuff right there. I remember thinking, *No, I did not know that! I must tell others! I don't think they know that either. My body's a temple? To be used by God?* **Wow.** *I didn't know.*

God cares about what *his* temple gets used for. I also read Jesus's words in Matthew 5:27–30:

> You have heard the commandment that says, "You must not commit adultery." But I say, anyone who even looks at a woman with lust has already committed adultery with her in his heart. So if your eye—even your good eye—causes you to lust, gouge it out and throw it away. It is better for you to lose one part of your body than for your whole body to be thrown into hell. And if your hand—even your stronger hand—causes you to sin, cut it off and throw it away. It is better for you to lose one part of your body than for your whole body to be thrown into hell.

This stuff was just rockin' my world. This Jesus I had completely fallen in love with was showing me he takes the whole purity thing pretty seriously, and he cares about every thought we let take up residence in our minds. The things my husband always wanted to talk about—pretending to be with other people and such things—was starting to mess with my mental and emotional life. I really just wanted to be intimate with my husband without the extra pictures on a computer screen or on the screen of our minds. I wanted to honor my God and my husband. And according to Jesus, the best thing I could do if something was causing me to stumble was to just cut it out of my life.

So I figured my husband would understand. I didn't want to participate in such things anymore. I wanted to be faithful to him and God even in my thought life. What husband wouldn't be grateful that his wife wants her thoughts to be only for him? I can't lie. I thought he would be so excited that his wife loved him so much, that he would have to resist the temptation to throw a parade in her honor. Let's just say there was no parade. Just the opposite. A storm of anger.

I didn't understand his response at all. I wasn't judging him; I was just trying to honor him. He was the one who first told me about Jesus and how we should honor him in all things. He started to be distant and cold to me. Then 9/11 happened.

I got up early the morning of 9/11 to spend time in the Word before I started my day. I was sitting in my maroon recliner, my place of solace ever since the time I couldn't breathe near the end of my first pregnancy. We (the recliner and I) have a lot of memories together. I rocked a lot of babies through a lot of early a.m.'s. I used to call it my recycling center, because it is where I would go when I felt completely empty and used up and had nothing left to give my wee ones. I would grab my One Year Bible and my journal and spend time with my Jesus. If things were really bad, I would be on my knees with my face smashed in the cushion praying. I would get up and feel transformed with a whole new resolve and purpose.

I am seriously missing that ugly, worn-out chair right now. We spent so much time together, and I hope it knows it was loved deeply.

So that is where I was when I heard my husband yell at me from the bedroom to come quickly. I turned the corner and saw one of the Twin Towers on fire. I sat in disbelief, watching the news when the second plane hit the other building. I remember my husband saying, "Oh my God, this means war."

The towers crashing down in a heap of rubble will forever mark our nation's history, and it will forever mark my life as well. I was about to go through a devastation in my marriage—one where I felt the towers of stability come down.

I wanted nothing more than to be held by my husband and have him tell me, "Even though the world seems crazy right now, it will be okay. We will get through it together." Instead, Scott seemed so angry with me and shut me out of his world altogether.

We watched a documentary about a New York fire department that was being filmed when 9/11 happened. They had video footage of all the firemen in one of the towers before they went up the stairs. My husband watched with tears in his eyes and anger in his heart for his fallen brothers. We laid in bed that night with the Grand Canyon between us. It was so lonely on my side of the canyon. I started to despair because I couldn't fix it.

I began reading books about how to fix marriages, communicate better with one another, and if you submit more to your husband, that will fix everything. (When dealing with addiction and someone who rages, more submission is **not** helpful, but we will get to that soon.) I remember having breakfast one morning with a pastor's wife at the time. I wouldn't share with her about the emotional abuse and other details of our marriage, because when I was first married, another pastor's wife told me, "Be careful who you tell, because you will forgive your husband of these things, but others will not." That stuck with me. I felt responsible for how people viewed my husband. I felt like a White House press secretary always doing damage control inside and outside the house.

That really was good advice and really bad advice all in one shot. Good advice because it is never of God for you to intentionally humiliate a person, publicly or privately. Bad advice because hidden sin rarely heals and just grows progressively worse. But God is about bringing out what happens in the dark into the light[2], not to hurt but to heal, and rescue people from a path that leads to death. The enemy does his best work in secret. *It does not mean you never go public, but before you do, check your motives with the Lord.* I do believe it is godly behavior to **not** always rescue people from life's consequences, and to be real with people in your life who have a history of a strong relationship with the Lord and wisdom to guide you in the right direction when dealing with such situations.

When questioned about how things were going in our marriage, I made general statements like, "Oh, we just aren't blending right now." One sweet, older lady started giving me advice. All I could think of was, *You have no idea what I live with. Your husband wouldn't raise his voice if he was on fire.* The week before, my husband stood over me while I was in the fetal position, f—ing me off while I cried, begging him to stop, to just please stop.

After that incident, I told him we needed to go to counseling, and I went to one of the pastors and told him what had happened. My husband agreed to go, not so much for me, but because of what the pastor might think of him if he didn't. I knew he didn't care about me, but he sure the heck cared about what people thought of him. So we went. I was able to share with Scott how, when he yelled at me and broke my possessions, it scared me. My husband's point of view was that it didn't happen all the time, so what was the big deal?

The pastor did a great job of trying to explain how it only has to happen one time and be so traumatic a person lives in constant fear of it happening again. I was sitting there thinking, *Yes, he gets it, exactly!* The pastor got it. Apparently, my husband did not. My husband was f—ing me off all the way home in the car. How dare I tell people our private business? I was trying my best to be the most godly, Christian wife I could be. I was reading marriage books, how-to-be-the-perfect-godly-wife books, and trying to put it all into practice, but things just kept spiraling downward.

Scott's other favorite form of retribution was to completely ignore me. Other than absolutely having to answer a question about our children's logistics, he would just stare straight ahead as if I weren't in the room or walk out altogether. This could go on for weeks.

Around this time, we had a new head pastor come to our church. I instantly connected with his wife. I remember our first breakfast together. I shared very generally that we had hit a rough spot in our marriage. I made sure to leave out how the other day, my husband tore apart the house because the house was messy. I had just finished making cookie trays for Christmas presents for the kids' teachers. My husband was getting off shift that morning, and I asked my mom to come over and help me catch up on getting the house picked up before he got home because I knew I was not within "the acceptable line."

Scott got home sooner than expected. I tried to get my mom out of the house because I could tell he was irritated. I quickly loaded up the cookie trays and kids to take the older one to kindergarten and the other two to preschool. I came home to all the laundry baskets dumped all over the place. I remember seeing laundry hanging on top of an open door in one of the kids' rooms. There was broken glass from a picture frame mixed in clothing in the hallway. My personalized wedding cake topper I had on display on top of our hallway cabinet was missing. The fireman had been torn off and thrown away, and I ended up throwing away the whole thing. Who wants a wedding cake topper with a lonely bride standing all alone on it? (Apparently, I do, because during a recent move, I found it! I guess I went back and grabbed it from the trash. I don't give up easily on people, even plastic ones!)

We had to attend our oldest child's kindergarten Christmas performance that morning. So I ignored the mess, changed, and drove back to our son's school, not knowing what else to do. Before leaving, I walked up to my husband and said, "I'm sure you weren't planning on it anyways, but make sure you don't sit by me at the school performance." That was it, my big boundary. We pretended in front of our neighbors at school that everything was great and went back home. I remember thinking, *I am not cleaning up this mess. He can do it!* But reality set in. I couldn't have kids and a toddler in the house with broken glass lying around. So I cleaned up the mess.

The new pastor's wife told me how impressed she was that I didn't tell her any details of our rough spot, that I was honoring my husband. It made me feel good she thought I was a good wife, protecting my husband from anyone thinking badly of him. I told her he was a really good man. He was just going through a rough time. He spent all his free time on the computer playing card games. However, I left out how furious he was with me because I didn't want to watch porn with him or pretend to do all sorts of ungodly scenarios, how he could go months without talking to me.

When my husband ignored me, I would spend my time reading the Bible, journaling, and reading big God stories. One of my favorites was *The Hiding Place*.[3] I remember praying, "Lord, could you make me brave like them?" When I read about Corrie ten Boom, I prayed, "Lord, if I ever live in a time like she did, would you please help me to be like Corrie and not put my personal safety above helping others?" Be careful what you pray for in your twenties. The Lord might take you up on that request in your forties and send you to Iraq! But I wouldn't want it any other way. Before that happened though, a whole lot of journaling from this overwhelmed, young mother happened.

I have journaled throughout most of our marriage, due to the fact that I really didn't know how to pray. Early on in my walk with God, all I knew about prayer was you are supposed to ask for God's will to be done and not yours and that God knows everything. I thought, *That doesn't leave much for us to talk about.* So not really knowing how to pray, I would just write letters to Jesus and talk with him like a trusted friend. I still do today. I have twenty-four years of letters to Jesus, and counting.

January 19

Hello, my Lord. Thank you for your peace. Things are not going well for my husband and me at all. Help us, Jesus, however you see fit. Thank you for being with me. I can't imagine life without you. Thank you for the time at the baby shower. It was a lot of fun. You are so good to me. You give me peace when I shouldn't have it. I love you, Jesus. Lord, I pray that you would make my husband and me into everything you created us to be. I almost don't want to stop writing because I feel such peace and contentment sitting here with you. Lord, please heal our marriage. I love you. In Jesus' name I pray.

January 21

Hello, my wonderful Father! Thank you for your wonderful peace. Things have been better in our marriage. For about the last few weeks, my husband has been very cold to me. I know he is stressed out over money and having to get his project done. He had a Fred moment the other day because I let our oldest put water in one of his toys. He was so angry with me. He seems like he is always frustrated with me. He is either at the fire station, at the office, or at home on the computer. He plays with the kids, but it is as if I don't exist. I wrote him an email about his Fred moments and how even though we may go back to normal living afterward, the scars are still there and the walls go up. He wrote me back and he ended it with saying, "You're not the only one who is putting up walls." Lord, I don't know what he has to put up walls about.

Lord, I am making a record of this season of our life because you, my Lord, are a faithful God who helps those who call upon your name. I know you hear my request to heal our marriage. Help us to grow closer together. Help us to enjoy each other's company. Help us to return to being best friends. You are the creator of all wonderful things. Create in us a new heart of love, compassion, and throw in some passion for each other while you're at it! Help me to be a loving and supportive wife. Make any changes necessary in us to make us into the couple you have created us to be. I love you, Jesus. I am excited to see what you will do in this situation. In Jesus' name I pray. Amen.

January 23

Hello, my Jesus. Thank you for strengthening me. Our middle little guy is sick with RSV. He had a really rough night last night. I did treatments every two hours. He had such a high fever; his body and head were wet. I thought he was going to start having a seizure. His eyes rolled to the back of his head and his tongue started to do I'm not sure what. It was only a couple of seconds. Then our oldest came home from school sick. He is sleeping on the floor now. It is 3:00 p.m. Our baby girl has a cold too. Lord, you are good; you are strengthening me. Help me to eat healthy, so I can stay energized and healthy to care for the kids. Please heal my family of their sickness. Thank you that I live in a country where we have medicine for my children. I am a blessed woman! Help me to work efficiently to keep up on housework and care for the children. Thank you, Jesus. You are amazing. In Jesus' name I pray. Amen.

The next night, a friend drove me to church, leaving my husband home with the sick kids. While at church, I suddenly felt the need to go home. I didn't want to bother my friend, so I asked another friend if she wouldn't mind driving me home right then, even though I couldn't explain why. When I arrived, my husband was making cupcakes in the kitchen and our asthmatic son was on the couch sleeping. I went over to check on him.

He was lethargic and struggling to breathe. I told my husband to come quickly. He loaded him in the car and drove him to the fire station while I stayed home with the other two kids.

January 25

Hello, my sweet Jesus. I am in the hospital with our middle son. Last night Scott took him to the fire station to check his O2 levels. He wasn't doing well. Scott called an ambulance. Our middle guy went code 3 (lights and sirens) to the hospital. We were at the ER until 3:30 a.m., then an ambulance took us to another ER. Finally, at 5:30 a.m., we got into our room. My little guy needs me to hold his oxygen mask now. Thank you, Jesus, for all your help and for family and friends. I love you. In Jesus' name. Amen.

My husband didn't believe in calling ambulances, so when I got the call from a fellow fire captain that Scott was going by ambulance, I knew my son was either dead or close to death. The fact that my husband had someone else make the call made me realize the seriousness of it. My dad had a little brother die at the age of four of an asthma attack, which was the same age my son was. An eleven-year-old girl had died in our area of an asthma attack around that same time. I remember driving to the ER and recalling a Scripture: "But you are holy, O you that inhabit the praises of Israel" (Psalm 22:3, NHEB).

A kind neighbor sat with my other two kids while I hurried to meet Scott. I remember going through the alphabet, saying an attribute of God for each letter as I drove to the hospital. I sat at the final red light across from the ER and said to the Lord, "I don't know if I am going to find out my son isn't still alive, but I give you my word, I will praise you regardless." It's strange. I was not in a hurry for the light to change. I just wanted to soak up a few more seconds with the Lord before I walked through the ER doors to face whatever was waiting for me. Seeing my husband's fire truck waiting outside the ER with the ambulance . . . everything was in slow motion.

January 25 (second entry)

Hello, my Father. Today is our baby girl's second birthday. Our middle guy might get out of the hospital tomorrow. I almost forgot today was our daughter's birthday with our little guy in the hospital. Scott said he is doing really good tonight. Thank you, Lord. You have provided for my every need. Today when I came home from the hospital to take a nap, I only had three messages and two were hang-ups. I started to get my feelings hurt, because last time our middle guy was in the hospital, we had an endless number of people calling to see if we needed anything or to share their concern for us. Lord, thank you for showing me how last time I had a bigger emotional need. This time I was just physically exhausted. Mentally, I was doing better. Help me, Lord, not to have hard feelings for that one friend not coming to the hospital the night my son went in the ambulance. Lord, you were with me. I know that for a fact. Although I was crying, I knew one way or another, everything would be OK because you were with me. I could talk to you forever, but I want to read your Word before I go to bed. I love you. In Jesus' name. Amen!

January 26

Lord, our marriage needs your help. Our communication is breaking down quick. Lord, I don't even feel like talking about it. We just need your help and quick.

When I traded places with Scott at the hospital, he wouldn't speak to me other than an exchange of medical facts that I needed to know. It crushed me. I didn't know what horrible thing I had done to make him so angry at me. Whatever it was, our son had almost died. Shouldn't that have put things in perspective of how short life is? There were no words for how alone I felt in my marriage.

January 26 (second entry)

Lord, thank you for our son being able to come home from the hospital today. Please continue to heal my children. Please,

Jesus, keep me and my family healthy. Help Scott and me not to get sick. Lord, you saw our conversation tonight. Things are not well. Help me, Jesus, to be faithful in praying for him. Lord, I pray your protection over our family and marriage. In Jesus' name. Amen. Give me peace.

In this next journal entry, I was sitting in my minivan, crying before walking into church, trying to get my "game face" on before entering. Before I did, I wanted to spend time journaling. I always felt the Lord's presence when I wrote him letters like I was talking to a close friend. This is what I wrote before walking into church.

January 27

Lord, help me. Help our family. It's falling apart. I'm getting ready to walk into church. Scott is at home with the kids. I'm trusting you, Lord, to sustain me and fix our marriage. You're my only hope. I am completely depending on you. I've tried talking with Scott, but he wants nothing to do with me. He called me an f—ing nun and a prude and... you know how it went. For the first time, he looked at me like he doesn't love me. Help me, Jesus. You are all I have. Please, Lord, have my family grow up in a complete, healthy family. I am waiting on you, Lord. We need a miracle. I would have never imagined we could get this bad. We used to be so good together. We made a great team. Help Scott. Deliver him, Jesus. In Jesus' name. Amen.

That night Scott told me I used to be fun in the bedroom, followed by, "I know what the problem is," and pointed to the very Bible he gave me when we were dating. All of this because I told him I was starting to struggle in my thought life because of all the things he kept wanting to expose me to in and out of the bedroom.

My "Christian" husband no longer wanted me to read the Bible because it was getting in the way of his "fun" wife. Porn corrupts the mind.

January 28

*Hello, my Jesus. Thank you for your peace. Scott and I haven't
spoken in days about anything other than necessary facts. Lord,
you have given me hope, peace, and even some joy when I have
no reason for it. You are amazing, and I am so thankful for you. I
will not believe the lies of Satan. He will not have victory in my
marriage. You brought us together, and we will not be torn apart.
I do not war against flesh and blood.[4] So Lord, equip me and
strengthen me for the fight ahead. Holy Spirit, guide me in my
prayer time. Victory is mine through Christ Jesus who strengthens
me. It is so cool, Lord, these are not just words but absolute truth.*

*Thank you, Jesus, for I know my future is good. You have plans to
give me a hope and a future.[5] You are an awesome God. Thank
you for my husband. I pray for deliverance for him. Free him in
Jesus' name. Thank you, Lord, for Psalm 55:16–18: "But I will
call on God, and the Lord will rescue me. Morning, noon, and
night I cry out in my distress, and the Lord hears my voice. He
ransoms me and keeps me safe from the battle waged against me,
though many still oppose me."*

January 29

*Lord, in the natural, my future does not look bright. I will take
captive every thought and put it under Christ Jesus. Lord, take
away the hardness of my heart and his. Obviously, I prefer you
work on him first, but I have a feeling that is not your game plan.
Lord, I submit my will to you. Please take away my anger and
desire to see Scott . . . I was going to say get some of his own, but
I don't mean it, Lord. I just want him to see how hurtful he can be
to me and at least be sorry or feel a little bad about it. Sometimes
living for you and trying to follow your example can be so hard at
times. Please forgive me, Jesus, for my unkind words.*

*You just reminded me, Lord, of the Scripture in Matthew 12:36,
"And I tell you this, you must give an account on judgment day*

for every idle word you speak." Lord, I want abundant heavenly
blessings for my husband. He is a good man. Free him from his
bondages, so he can be the man you created him to be. Lord, you
brought us together as a team to be used by you—change us both,
Lord. Bind Satan and kick him out of our marriage. In Jesus'
name. Amen.

Things improved somewhat for a little while, only to return to Fred time a month or so later, which had a grand finale of what I call my "beautiful breakdown." The toughest day of my life produced the most beautiful results. As my hero in the faith Corrie Ten Boom once said, "You can never learn that Christ is all you need, until Christ is all you have."[6] When I wrote some of these journal entries, it never entered my mind for a second that anyone but Jesus would ever read them. "This is what the past is for! Every experience God gives us, every person He puts in our lives is the perfect preparation for the future that only He can see."[7] I had to walk through Isaiah 45:3: "And I will give you treasures hidden in the darkness—secret riches. I will do this so you may know that I am the Lord, the God of Israel, the one who calls you by name."

I was about to go through the darkest night of my life. But God was there waiting for me.

8

MY DARKEST NIGHT

"Darkness is all around me; thick, impenetrable darkness is everywhere."

JOB 23:17

I WANTED to leave my husband. I figured if he hated me so much, let's just call this thing now and get a divorce. Being in the same house with him day after day, being treated as though he hated me, was breaking me down. Sometimes God doesn't deliver us from our problems but walks with us through them. God interrupted my plan of leaving my husband.

I began reading a book called *Jesus Freaks*. The entire book is filled with stories of men and women who loved and trusted the Lord with such passion that their tough life circumstances seemed to only strengthen them instead of weakening them. The Lord gave those persecuted Christians supernatural peace in their circumstances. These stories were messing with my mind in a whole new way. Could God do the same for me? I did argue with the Lord how in these stories the Christians were trying to share the love of Jesus with their unsaved persecutors. I, on the other hand, had married a Christian, and I shouldn't have to do this!

Then I read a story about two Chinese girls who used their last words on earth to encourage their pastor who took their lives.

Flanked by renegade guards, the executioner came with a revolver in his hand. It was their own Pastor! He had been sentenced to die with the two girls. But, as on many other occasions in church history, the persecutors worked on him, tempting him. They promised to release him if he would shoot the girls. He accepted. The girls whispered to each other, then bowed respectfully before their pastor. One of them said, "Before you shoot us, we wish to thank you heartily for what you've meant to us. You baptized us, you taught us the ways of eternal life, you gave us holy communion with the same hand in which you now hold the gun. You also taught us that Christians are sometimes weak and commit terrible sins, but they can be forgiven again. When you regret what you are about to do to us, do not despair like Judas, but repent like Peter. God bless you, and remember that our last thought was not one of indignation against your failure. Everyone passes through hours of darkness. May God reward you for all the good you have done to us. We die with gratitude." They bowed again. The pastor's heart was hardened. He shot the girls. Afterwards, he was shot by the communists.[1]

*Please let me add that I was not concerned for my physical safety. If you are in any physical danger, **please** seek help immediately. Even Paul took advantage of his legal protections afforded to him by Roman law when he was going to be beaten. If you live in a country that has laws to protect you, please use them. Paul did and he was a very brave, obedient man of God. (see Acts 22:22–29)*

The Lord just kept asking me, "Do you love me?"

"Yes!" I would answer. "You know I love you."

The Lord told me, "If you mean what you say about loving me, you will show him unconditional love."

The story of the Chinese girls has affected me profoundly. They used their last words, their last breath, to encourage the one who was taking their lives. Such compassion and grace. I will forever be grateful for their example and hope to meet them one day in heaven. Their example played a huge role in our family history.

"Blessed are the meek, for they will inherit the earth." (Matthew 5:5, NIV) I struggled with thinking that God was calling me to be a "weak" woman. I had never really understood the verse, until I looked up the word meekness. I love how the illustrated dictionary of the Bible defines it: "Meekness is an attitude of humility toward God and gentleness toward men, springing from a recognition that God is in control."[2] God wasn't calling me to be a weak woman but to be a *meek* woman. Although weakness and meekness may look similar, they are not. Weakness has a negative connotation, such as a lack of strength or lack of courage. But meekness is due to a person's conscious choice. "It's strength and courage under control, coupled with kindness."[3]

I like how Eugene Bach put it in *Jesus in Iran*:

Blessing your enemy is not to be confused with passive ministry. This does not mean there will not be confrontations, and it does not mean that there will not be fierce opposition. Blessing and loving are not the same as appeasement. Appeasement is the opposite of love. Appeasement is essentially about self-preservation. Love, true love, is willing to be sacrificial.[4]

Up until this point, I was about appeasement for self-preservation.

May 5

Oh, my Jesus. I need your comfort now! I feel like my husband has ice running through his veins. I felt like you told me in church you were going to walk me through with your unconditional love. I know for a fact I can't do it in my own strength. Lord, my hope is in you. There is no hope for my marriage in the natural. You're the only one who can give us a testimony of restoration. Help me, Jesus. I do ask, Lord, that you would please help me, give me your supernatural peace. Lord, please heal my children of their fevers. Give us health. I'm speaking Saturday at the mother-

daughter banquet. Help me, Jesus. I love you. Change Scott's and my heart to your perfect will. In Jesus' name I pray.

I once heard a man speak at our church. He would take a life-size cross into different countries to share Jesus with people. He had so many miraculous stories of God's provision and protection. One of the things he said stuck with me: "What do you do when God calls you to a country and war breaks out? Do you still go? Yes. God's call is not determined by life's circumstances."

While listening to his sermon on a trip, I felt like the Lord was going to ask me to speak at our church again. When I returned from my trip that weekend, the pastor's wife came up to me and asked if I would speak at the mother-daughter tea that year. She said all the ladies requested me.

This was my second speaking engagement at my church. The first one was the year prior when I ran off stage after looking at the crowd, getting scared, and crying. I said, "Oh my goodness, I am so sorry. This really sucks, and you guys paid to be here," and ran off stage and cried at the bottom of the stage. Someone told me it could've been worse. I could've just passed out. I told them that would have been so much better because it was a charismatic church, and they would have thought God was really moving!

Apparently, God really meant Romans 11:29: "For God's gifts and his call can never be withdrawn." Because why anyone would ask me to speak after that makes no human sense at all!

I share the following journal entries for a few reasons. I have had women look at my husband and me and say, "I wish I could have a marriage like yours." People who have known us for years kind of smirk because they know the road we have had to walk. It's true! Our marriage is pretty awesome today, and I trust Jesus for tomorrow's victory. But before the awesome kicked in, there was a whole lot of the awful. (Is it wrong that Pat Benatar's song, "Love Is a Battlefield," is playing in my mind right now?)

May 6

Hello, my Jesus. You are my everything. Thank you, Lord, for giving me a break and giving Scott overtime (getting him out of the house). Help me to use today to strengthen myself in you. Help me, Jesus. Refresh me. Do a miracle in our lives. Please deliver Scott from his anger. Help him. Release him in Jesus' name from his bondages. Draw him back to you, Lord. I don't know how you should or could do it. But you are God; all things are possible for you, Christ Jesus. Help him to be the on-fire-for-Jesus, loving person you created him to be. Lord, help me to support him in the way he needs. I love you, Jesus. Please give me peace in spite of my circumstances. In Jesus' name. Amen.

Oh, what a battle it was. Psalm 30:5b says, "Weeping may last through the night (or in my case, several nights), but joy comes with the morning." (addition mine) It couldn't come soon enough.

May 10

(4:30 a.m.) Hello, my Jesus. My sweet girl woke up. I can't seem to fall back to sleep. I keep trying to figure out what to say Saturday. Lord, I know you will be with me. This is such a growing time for me. As you know, I am not enjoying it, but I know you will use it for good. I love you. Please help me to fall back asleep at least until 6:00. In Jesus' name I pray.

(5:20 a.m.) Oh, my sweet Jesus, comfort me with your peace. I am filled with anxiety. I surrender it all to you. Fill me with your supernatural peace.

(12:00 p.m.) Hello, my Jesus, I'm waiting for my son's kindergarten bus. Thank you, Jesus, for praying friends. Sandy prayed with me this morning. You granted me peace.

(9:15 p.m.) Hello, my Jesus. Thank you for helping me through the day. Please help me to relax and just enjoy the opportunity to

talk about you. I love you, Jesus. Please change Scott's heart and mine. I love you. In Jesus' name. Amen.

(11:51 p.m.) My sweet, amazing Jesus, please grant me peace and rest tonight. Jesus, my Lord, is wonderful! Come, sweet, peaceful Jesus, and soothe my soul and relax and comfort my body in Jesus' name I pray.

May 11

(12:50 a.m.) Lord, don't let me forget who I am in you. I was created to encourage your people. I am perfectly equipped to accomplish everything you have called me to be. I will walk in the confidence of being your daughter. I am the precious daughter of the King of kings and the Lord of lords. I will walk in the calling you have given me. May your anointing fall upon me. In the name of Jesus, I command the voice of the enemy to be silent. I cast out all fear and doubt. In Jesus' name. Thank you, Jesus, for my perfect peace. I am your precious daughter. I will act and walk out a life of royalty. God has already won the victory for me. I receive it in Jesus' name. Amen.

The next two entries were written in shaky handwriting.

(4:15 a.m.) Hello, my Jesus, my sweet, gentle Father. Lord, peace is eluding me. Help me, Jesus. Help me, Jesus. You are God. Bring peace to this trembling body. I love you, Jesus. You are my shield and my strength; you are my comforter. My provider, you are perfect. You are my everything, and you are the giver of great gifts. Your love is everlasting. You are slow to anger, full of mercy. You are Abba, Father. You are my rock. You are my Savior. I love you, Jesus. Praise your holy name; You are worthy of all praises. Thank you, Jesus for being with me. My strength is in you.

(6:00 a.m.) Thank you, Jesus. I have made it through the night. I am so weak, Lord. I am grateful for morning. No one can bring

me comfort but you, Jesus. You are the only comforter of my soul. Give me peace, Jesus. Jesus, let me walk out your will in perfect peace. I give you my obedience. I love you, Jesus. I submit my will to you, Lord. I will walk in confidence in you! In Jesus' name.

I left to go speak feeling so weak. I didn't even have the strength to shower. When I arrived, I had never felt so alone in my whole life. Our country was preparing for war; there were anthrax scares; my son was continually being hospitalized; and I was a mother of three young kids and had a husband who despised her and made sure she knew it. It sucked.

I walked into a roomful of women ready to celebrate Mother's Day. This time, I gave God my word I would not step off that stage until I had spoken the word he had given me. I realized I didn't have the strength to deliver the funny message I knew the ladies were expecting. They didn't know that Anna was completely broken, but they were about to find out.

My brokenness and weakness were on display that morning. As I walked up to the stage, I had these words in my head: "Do you still go? Yes . . ." War had broken out in my life, but I had never been more sure that I was supposed to show up and deliver that message. It would not be wrapped up in humor nor funny anecdotes, just raw obedience wrapped in weakness. I did not deliver the message I had originally prepared that would have been a cotton-candy-filled pep talk.

"The Lord has been speaking a lot to me about obedience. Obedience even during what feels like the most difficult situations. Even if you feel like it's killing you." (I didn't share with them exactly what I was going through, only that it was a really rough time.) "I've been reading this book called *Jesus Freaks*. It's about people remaining faithful to Jesus even unto death. Just like when Jesus asked Peter three consecutive times, 'Peter, do you love me?' I keep hearing the Lord asking me the same question lately. Will I stay and be obedient even when it is painful? I believe the Lord is asking someone here today the same question."

I read the story from *Jesus Freaks* about the Chinese girls. I stepped off the stage and felt the joy of obedience. A year earlier, when I was preparing to speak for that first event that felt like a big heaping failure, I asked the Lord why I was so nervous about speaking. I felt like he told me, "You are nervous because you really believe your destiny is determined by your performance instead of your obedience." That is why when people ask me after I speak somewhere, "How did it go?," I answer based on whether or not I was obedient to what I felt the Lord had asked me to do, not whether I felt like I had performed well. That Mother's Day luncheon wasn't pretty in the natural, but I knew I had been obedient.

As soon as I got back to my chair, my pastor's wife handed me a napkin with a Scripture reference on it: "Everyone has heard about your obedience, so I rejoice because of you." (Romans 16:19a, NIV) Of course, that made me cry. The thought of God rejoicing because of me! I was so happy. I had managed to be obedient even though I was so scared to speak in front of those ladies.

I believe in a thing called "spiritual warfare," frankly because the Bible talks about it, but also because I have experienced it. Ephesians 6:12: "For we are not fighting against flesh-and-blood enemies, but against evil rulers and authorities of the unseen world, against mighty powers in this dark world, and against evil spirits in the heavenly places." After a big life victory, what you may have thought was the finish line to your testing, was not. When you tell yourself, "If I can just make it to this point or get to this line, then things will be better," but just when you get to that line, you find somehow it got pushed back even further. I really felt if I could just make it through the Mother's Day brunch, the enemy would be defeated—the battle would be over.

May 11

It is finished! Thank you, Jesus! I spoke today at the mother-daughter luncheon. It did not go smoothly, but I know I was obedient to you. It feels good, Lord, to be free! I love you, Jesus! I am grateful for you.

Later in the night, while Scott was working a twenty-four-hour shift at the station, I journaled with a trembling hand.

May 12

(3:15 a.m.) Help me, Jesus. Let my body know what it is to have peace. Thank you for the friends that came over at midnight to pray with me. They left at 1:00 a.m. Thank you for my wonderful friends. Lord, I feel like you're not hearing me. My body cannot find peace.

I called one of my older-than-me (physically and spiritually) friends to come over and sit with me after journaling that. It's hard to imagine now, but I was so filled with fear and despair I honestly didn't think I had the strength to get through the night. My friend sang worship songs over me while I laid on the couch. Thank God for faithful friends. I wouldn't be here today without them.

"Two people are better off than one, for they can help each other succeed. If one person falls, the other can reach out and help. But someone who falls alone is in real trouble," and "A person standing alone can be attacked and defeated, but two can stand back-to-back and conquer. Three are even better, for a triple-braided cord is not easily broken." Ecclesiastes 4:9–10, 12.

Why is it you can feel so confident in the daytime, but when nighttime rolls around, the sky isn't the only thing dark, but life circumstances feel darker? Doubt and fear breed so easily when alone in the dark. At the time, I felt like I was the only one who ever doubted if God really knew what was going on in my life or if he was even hearing me. I didn't know it at the time, but I was far from being the first person to doubt in the darkness what they knew to be true in the light.

John the Baptist shook the established system. He showed no fear of man, calling it like it was. He called out Jesus for who he was, the long-awaited Messiah who was foretold from the prophets of old. He was the one who baptized Jesus, and while doing so, John recognized exactly who Jesus was.

"After his baptism, as Jesus came up out of the water, the heavens were opened and he saw the Spirit of God descending like a dove and settling on him. And a voice from heaven said, "This is my dearly loved Son, who brings me great joy." Matthew 3:16–17.

Wow! I can't imagine!

If anyone had nailed down Jesus' identity, it would have been John the Baptist. But shortly after this encounter, we find out John's lack of people-pleasing skills won him some powerful enemies. Apparently, some people didn't like it when he called them out on their sexual sins.

Making a stand for Jesus and his standards can cost a person. And even a strong person who doesn't back down to anyone, the kind of person like John, can even start to question things he was once so sure of. Once he found himself trapped in a dark prison, things that were once nailed down in the light ("Jesus is the Messiah we have been waiting for") went from being solidly planted in his mind to need reassurance from Jesus.

John sent his disciples to ask Jesus if he was the Messiah or if they should keep looking for someone else. Jesus gave him this answer: "Then he told John's disciples, 'Go back to John and tell him what you have seen and heard—the blind see, the lame walk, those with leprosy are cured, the deaf hear, the dead are raised to life, and the Good News is being preached to the poor.'" (Luke 7:22)

I believe John started struggling, hearing about all the amazing things Jesus was capable of, and probably started to ask, "What about me and my situation?" After all, look how faithful he'd been to him. But instead of a rescue, Jesus sent a message back to John: "God blesses those who do not fall away because of me." (Luke 7:23)

Jesus was encouraging John not to turn away when he didn't show up for him the way John thought he should.

I, too, was starting to question during my dark night of the soul. Why wouldn't God deliver me? I'd heard and read about his amazing delivering power. I had done everything I knew how to do. Why wouldn't he do that for me?

9

BEAUTIFUL BREAKDOWN

INSTEAD OF A RESCUE from my circumstances, Jesus had a message waiting for me the very next day. I wouldn't receive that message just yet though. First, I had to take a trip to the urgent care. I hadn't slept or eaten much over the previous week. Thankfully, the Lord helped me realize I needed some medical intervention.

I am a pretty severe hypoglycemic girl. If I go too long without eating, I get the shakes and have a hard time keeping down the very thing my body needs—food. I realized I needed to get some medical help so I could keep down nourishment. Getting support for that decision can be a challenge in some Christian communities who view seeking medical help as a sign of lacking trust in God.

I was so overcome with anxiety and fear, I thought this was what hell must feel like—complete terror and believing God is not coming for you. I was picturing me and the kids homeless. I was fearing everything! I feared staying and leaving. I wanted out, but the Lord was asking me to stay.

Every day seemed like a battle to get through. I was twenty-nine years old with three kids, ages six and under, and one of them needing breathing treatments around the clock. Watching the daily news of the World Trade Center rubble being cleaned up and hearing stories of people's lives devastated added stress and anxiety. I was about to break. The thought of living alone and unloved by my husband was too much to bear.

I went to church on Mother's Day in hopes of finding someone willing to drive me the thirty minutes to the urgent care and who wouldn't tell me to go home and pray more. I found the pastor's wife and a girlfriend who agreed I should go see a doctor. My concerns about people thinking I shouldn't seek help were unfounded. The Lord provided abundantly for me that day. My pastor's wife asked me to attend just the worship part of the service so I could be prayed for before leaving. I went and sat in the front row.

While praying over me, the pastor asked the Lord to give me peace regardless of the outcome. It was so simple. But the Lord used it to change something in my thinking. Up until then, my whole existence was asking God to give me peace while waiting for my husband to come out of depression or darkness. You could see there was darkness in his eyes, a coldness that just kept getting worse. His heart was so hard. I told a girlfriend, "I feel like I'm dying of emotional cancer. I'm on the floor reaching out to my husband for help, and his response is a 'can you please go die in the corner—you are in my way here.'" My whole prayer was based on giving me strength *until* my husband came out of it so I could go back to being OK. Why wasn't God fixing him so I could be OK? That way of thinking equaled complete despair and breakdown.

As the pastor was praying, it occurred to me for the first time, what if I prayed instead that the Lord would give me peace regardless of what my husband did? Whether he loved me or didn't love me. Instead of "Please, Lord, I *need* him to love me."

After the prayer, off to urgent care I went. It was very humbling having to stand in line, then walking up to the counter and trying to whisper so the others didn't hear me say, "I need help. I have some things going on in my life, and I'm not dealing with them very well." I went and sat down with my friend. Oh, thank you, Jesus, for friends! I waited for my name to be called.

While we were at the doctor's, another friend of mine had her fireman husband go and try to talk with Scott. They had known each other for years, and her husband was a believer as well. On the drive home, I called my friend to see how the visit went. Her husband just asked what was going on and told Scott his wife was being driven to urgent care right then. He said Scott didn't seem to care. That hurt. I still couldn't figure out what I had done to make him feel this way about me. I would do anything for him. Well, almost anything except agree to sin against God with him.

I returned home in a drug-induced peace. What I really needed, and craved, was a long-lasting, non-drug-induced peace. The kind I believe only Jesus can give. During this time I thought the only way to obtain this elusive peace I so desperately desired was for my husband to love me again, or for me to leave my lack-of-peace problem, my husband. But God had a very different lasting solution to my problem.

While starting to come out of my drug-induced state, my kids came and circled my recliner, tugging on me, saying, "Mommy, I'm hungry." I was still too drugged to have the strength to fix them something to eat. This was the first time I had ever questioned God since coming to know him. I remember saying, "God, do you even see me? Do you even care that I can't even feed my children?" Right in the middle of questioning God's faithfulness, my doorbell rang. (I can hardly tell this part of my story without tears filling my eyes.) I got up, answered the door, and a friend was standing there. She said, "Sorry to bother you, but we tried calling. We were just wondering if it would be okay to take your kids out for hamburgers."

How did they know? I was just questioning if God even cared that I didn't have the strength to feed my children! Of course, they didn't know, but God knew! Once again, he sent ridiculous provision, as he has done throughout my life.

While my kids were at their heavenly provided dinner, the Lord had life-changing work in mind for me. I stared out the window, watching my husband mow the lawn. I no longer blamed God for me getting this low. He had just proven how much he cared for me, but I still blamed my husband. After all, who wouldn't have anxiety attacks living with that angry man! As I watched my husband, I said to myself, "I hate you. This is all your fault that I have gotten to this point." In that moment, just like with John the Baptist, instead of a rescue from my circumstances, God sent me a message.

I felt like he told me, "My daughter, nowhere in my Word does it say, 'Scott is the giver of peace.' You are where you are because you have taken your eyes off me." In that moment, I came to the complete end of myself and surrendered everything to the Lord.

I had been reading about this guy named Paul in the Bible. He and his friend Silas were just thrown in jail because they had freed a young girl from a demon that had used her for evil. Her owners were making money from her, and when that was gone, they incited the crowd against them. (see Acts 16:16–40)

I was still fairly new to God's Word, and reading about these great men being thrown in jail was shocking to me. Obviously, I wasn't dealing well with being "persecuted" for desiring to honor God publicly and behind closed doors. Now I knew—expect to be attacked when you mess with or question someone's power or prosperity. All I knew at the time was I was doing my best to honor God and be a godly wife, and it was not turning out awesome so far.

Paul and Silas were wrongly imprisoned; they did not deserve to be there. Freeing a girl from a demon should've earned them a parade of gratefulness, but instead, it earned them a stay in prison. I felt I, too, had tried to honor God and found myself trapped in prison. The only difference was my prison didn't have four walls but was still a cage of fear. I just couldn't seem to break out. But God had a plan to free Paul, Silas, and even the jailer! It all started with Paul and Silas singing and worshiping and refusing to take their eyes off Jesus. Jesus also had a plan to free me as well. Thank you, Jesus!

Standing in front of that window, I told the Lord, "I have asked you to change my husband for the last seven years. I can't seem to get you on board with that, so you know what, change *me*. Show me how to have peace when there is no peace in my household. I keep reading about this guy, Paul, in your Word. He actually said he had learned to be content and at peace with everything—even with being in danger of being killed! You know what, Lord, this is no longer about you changing my husband.

I want to know if this peace you gave Paul is real. Lord, I ask you to do that same thing for me."

If God's Word is true, then I wanted him to show me. It was as if until this moment, I had been holding a five lb. weight in each outstretched arm. Not that hard to do for a little while but unbearable after a long time. The only thing that could make it OK for me to put those hand weights down was my husband loving me again. It took a nervous breakdown to finally realize I could no longer hold the responsibility of whether my husband loved me. I decided the weights were too heavy for me and set them down in the corner and told the Lord they were his. He could have them. They were too heavy and exhausting for me to carry.

Later in my quiet time with the Lord, I felt like he wanted me to ask a couple friends to come over and help me clean my house and get it in order. I really didn't want to because one time when my son was getting out of the hospital, some ladies from my Bible study group came over to help me get my house clean and dusted. The following week, one of the ladies made jokes about how messy it was. I kindly told the Lord, "No way. I am way too emotionally fragile right now to go down that path again. Besides, a clean house feels like it would be a reward to my husband."

Shortly after this conversation with the Lord, my phone rang. It was my sweet friend who drove me to the hospital. She asked, "Would you please pray about allowing me and two of my friends to come over to your house and clean it for you? Just to be a blessing to you. We would really love to do that if it's OK." I told her, "You're not going to believe this, but this morning in my quiet time, I felt like the Lord wanted me to call and ask for help, but I told him no. I don't want people seeing my house messy or my life in general messy. So, yes. Thank you for the fresh start." They came over and were a blessing, physically and emotionally.

May 13

Thank you, Jesus! I am doing so much better today. I was able to sleep last night and took a nap today and I have been able to eat. Thank you, Jesus. You are so faithful.

Even though there were times when I couldn't feel you this week, I know you were there for me. Thank you for all of the wonderful friends you have provided for me. I love you and want to serve you. In Jesus' name.

I learned another valuable lesson during this time about the importance of taking care of not only my spiritual life, but my physical body as well. When you are facing high stress, it is important to make sure you are fueling your body with things that will strengthen you for the battle. Although my mind-set and prayers were headed in a new direction, my body was not. I had neglected that part, and it also played a part in me physically and emotionally breaking down. I love how the Word once again shows us we aren't the first ones to break down and despair. Some mighty men of God who came before us could relate.

In 1 Kings 18, we read about Elijah in the great "Who's the Real God?" showdown. One of my favorite parts of the story is when Elijah started taunting the prophets of Baal, saying they needed to shout louder. With a little sarcastic "Perhaps he is daydreaming, or is relieving himself" (v. 27) brightens my day. Having a little humor, a bathroom joke no less, while your life's on the line . . . it makes me smile.

Good news: he won that battle hands down. Unfortunately, I don't think he finished one victory lap before his courage tank pegged E. He went from brave hero, to on-the-run zero in the span of one chapter. One message from Jezebel was the proverbial straw that broke his poor camel's back. "Then he went on alone into the wilderness, traveling all day. He sat down under a solitary broom tree and prayed that he might die. 'I have had enough, Lord,' he said. 'Take my life, for I am no better than my ancestors who have already died.'" (1 Kings 19:4)

Elijah needed a nap, food, nap again, and the Lord woke him up to tell him in verse 7: "Then the angel of the Lord came again and touched him and said, 'Get up and eat some more, or the journey ahead will be too much for you.'"

When you are in the midst of a hard journey, be sure to take care of your physical needs. It is doctor/Bible recommended.

In my mind, I was determined to follow Paul and Silas's example. I would find things I could be thankful for and focus on those things instead of wondering if my husband would talk with me that day.

The next morning, my body was still feeling nervous, so I was in the restroom with stomach issues. As I was reading about David and Saul's attempts to kill him, I started wondering if David's nerves ever got the best of him and he got stomach issues. Oh man, that would be horrible; they didn't have toilet paper or indoor plumbing. I looked up to my right and sitting there was a brand-new, *huge*, warehouse-sized pack of toilet paper. That was my thankful starting point. I thought, *Do you realize how many women around the world don't have the privilege of toilet paper? Here I am with something like forty rolls! I am so blessed!*

It actually made me laugh, thinking what a pitiful gratitude starting point: toilet paper. It didn't feel like a lot was going right with my life. I had to work with what I had. And what I had was a whole lot of toilet paper!

A while later, one of my friends from high school called, and my husband answered the phone. When I got on the phone with her, the first words out of her mouth were, "What is going on with your husband? He doesn't sound like himself." I shared with her, "You just heard him happy. That was a lot better than I've heard him lately." She suggested we come up for a visit, that maybe we just needed to get away for a weekend. So we did. It was primarily a nice getaway with the exception of an awkward moment where she and her husband shared that someone we went to high school with was in a *Playboy* magazine and brought the issue out to show us. My stomach dropped. *No, not here too, Lord! What am I supposed to do?* She showed us the picture, and I told her I didn't recognize her . . . any part of her.

I then defaulted to what I do best and changed the subject to, "Let's eat. I'm hungry. Where are we going for dinner?" I handed the magazine back to my friend, and she called me a prude. Everyone laughed, and I excused myself to the restroom. My husband came in and saw I was upset. I told my husband, "I'm not a prude. Sorry, I just don't want that in my life anymore." He made a joke and said I just didn't hear her right. She didn't call me a prude but a prune. It made me laugh and lightened the mood. That was the first care or concern he had shown me in such a long time. Other than that, we had a nice weekend.

We were able to talk on the drive home. I felt like, for the first time in a while, we heard each other. I shared with him I could understand him a lot better if he would talk to me instead of yelling and cursing at me. I gave him the example of how I knew he could control it because he would never talk to the fire chief like that, and he didn't even like him. All I was asking for was the same respect he'd give to a man he couldn't stand. He said he would try and do better.

May 20

Hello, my sweet Jesus. You are amazing. Thank you for a wonderful time in Las Vegas with my husband. Thank you for the opportunity to talk with him on the way home. I love you, Jesus. Help me to be stronger, Lord. I want my stability to come from you. Change me and use me for your glory.

Even though there were hints of progress, we still had a ways to go. Scott still would emotionally check out by being on the computer for hours at a time.

May 21

Hello, Jesus. Thank you for today. I know I am being petty, but I do not like my husband right now. He plays online card games all the time. I went to take the trash out tonight. It was really heavy, so I dragged it, and when I went to lift it into the barrel, the bottom fell out. The entire bag of trash on the ground. I went and told him what happened, told him he could help if he wanted. He said he would, but he didn't. He just continued to play cards. I got all the kids tucked in bed while he continues to play his online

*card game. I love you, Jesus, but I'm finding it hard to like him
right now.*

Although my husband continued to emotionally check out, my Father in heaven did not. God continued to show me his presence during this difficult time through other answered prayers.

On May 28, I journaled about how it was hard for me to get rid of our high chair. All three of our kids used the same one, and our daughter had outgrown it. It was time, since she was the grand finale. But I attach emotions to objects, because why wouldn't you? Other than the fact you don't want your house to look like a thrift store. So I prayed, "Lord, the only way I can get myself to release this is knowing it would be helping someone else. Let this be an answer to someone's prayers."

I dragged it out in front of our house because we lived across from a busy walking route around a lake. I couldn't stand to see it go and drug it back in, then out, then in, then out again. Luckily, the phone rang. By the time I hung up, the high chair was gone. It wasn't too long after that I was visiting one of the ladies from church who lived not too far from me. She walked me into the kitchen and showed me the high chair I had placed on the curb and told me, "You are not going to believe how good God is. I had been praying the Lord would help me find an inexpensive high chair for when I watch my grandchildren. One night when I went for a walk, someone had put this in front of their house with a free sign on it! Can you believe that? Isn't God amazing?"

I could hardly let her finish her story to tell her it was my kids' high chair, and I had prayed it would go to a good home. This simple event and others like it just made me feel seen by God, even if I was going through a rough time. I have so many answered prayers I would have forgotten if I hadn't journaled about it.

May 29

*Hello, Jesus. Right this very second, my oldest son (in
kindergarten) is starting his very own prayer journal! Thank you,
Jesus! Lord, let him always love you and serve you. Help my
other two also be passionate for you.*

Today, when my oldest came home from school, he had a surprise for me. He had saved up his allowance for a couple of weeks to buy me a ring. I love it! That ring means as much to me as my wedding ring. It was given to me with so much love! He ran into the house and told me to close my eyes while he got something out of his backpack. It is a gold ring with gold petals and a pink bead in the middle. God, you are so good to me! I love you.

June 3

Hello, Jesus. It is summertime. Not my favorite time of the year. I don't enjoy the long days. Trying to get the kids settled at night so I can spend time with you is challenging to say the least. I wanted to thank you, Lord, that I saw that my husband brought two books home. One had to do with anger management and the other on love relationships. I don't know if they are his or someone lent them to him. Thank you, Jesus. You love him even more than I do. Thank you for working in our lives. I love you, Jesus.

During that year, my husband decided I wasn't going to be the only one he was angry with. He and my dad always enjoyed each other's company before. But now, he avoided my parents and was cold or rude to them when he did see them. I remember my dad asking me privately, "What's going on with your husband. Did we do something to offend him?"

All I could tell him was the truth. "Dad, I don't know what is going on with him this last year. We have been having a rough time. Sorry for how he treats you guys; you don't deserve it. I don't know what to do."

I will be forever grateful to my parents for not putting extra pressure on me. I will always remember my dad's response. "Don't you worry about us. We love your husband. Just take care of yourself and your marriage. Let us know if you need help. We will be praying for you." My dad rarely, if ever, said, "I'll be praying for you." This was one of those times.

June 8

Hello, my Jesus. I am a blessed woman. You amaze me, Lord, that you would be so generous to me. I have a wonderful family. Thank you, Jesus, for my children. I love them so much. They are all so different. They have good hearts. Thank you, Jesus. I had no idea how cool being a mom would be. Thank you for my husband. Thank you that he loves you. Please help him to grow into your perfect will. Please heal the relationship between him and my parents. Soften his heart toward them. Help me, Lord, to do your perfect will in this situation. Help me to speak to him about this only if it is your will. Lord, I know you have a plan for all of this, so just let me know where or if you need me to be a part of it. I love you. In Jesus' name I pray.

~

My mother-in-law once shared with me how Scott's father would beat her for no reason. As she was putting Scott in his crib as a baby, she remembered her husband coming up and hitting her and busting her ear drum. I asked her, "There is *never ever* an excuse for that, but what in his mind was the reason?" She said, "I don't know—just keep me in line." I learned on a family camping trip that it was not a few isolated beatings she endured, but all the way up until the end, when her husband left her and married one of his mistresses.

My husband had told me how his dad cheated on his mom frequently but never about the physical abuse. I thought maybe it must have just happened when he was a baby and didn't remember it. So on one of the times during our 9/11 year, I shared with him what his mom had told me. He started to cry and yelled at me, "I know what my dad was! I don't need you to tell me." I went over to hug him, but he pushed me away, sucked up his tears, and replaced it with his stone-cold face. That was it. The only glimpse into the pain hidden behind cold, angry eyes.

~

Ever since a car accident right before we got married, I have had terrible migraines and shoulder pain. As we were vacationing at an oceanfront, my niece was rubbing Icy Hot on my shoulder to help with the pain. We were inside the motorhome when Scott yelled at me to get out of there and go help with the kids. It frustrated me that he was insensitive to my pain. I told him I was sorry I wasn't out there, but I didn't understand how three adults couldn't handle three children without me for a few minutes. He yelled at me in front of his family and finished it with, "Why don't you just go and drown yourself in that ocean?"

I walked away from Scott. I was so embarrassed. Usually, Scott would control himself and only treat me that way in private. It felt extra embarrassing to have it on display for others to see. Just the previous day at Sea World, Scott became angry at me for bringing a whole can of formula in the diaper bag. "Why would you do that? It takes up too much space. There is no way the baby is going to need all that formula! You should have just put some in a smaller container. Now we have to have this heavy bag with us all day."

My thought process was the bag just hangs on the stroller. No one is carrying it. What's the big deal? It's better than risking not having enough and nowhere to buy any.

Scott didn't talk to me for half the day. It was getting old. But ignoring me when I did something he didn't like, making me "pay," felt like some type of prison sentence where I was sent to isolation. That is, until I would go and spend time with the Lord. I'm not trying to make myself sound spiritual; I was just so desperate. I truly did find Jesus to be a safe refuge.

July 2

Oh, my Jesus, thank you for a great day. I didn't feel like losing my temper that much today. What a difference it makes spending time with you. Tonight I was being lazy, lying out on the trampoline when my oldest said to me, "Mom, if everyone in the world was really nice, everyone would be fighting." I told him, "No, they wouldn't be fighting. If everyone was really nice, there would be no reason for fighting." He said, "Yes they would. They

*would be saying, "No, you can have it. No, you have it. No, you
have it." It was so cute. Lord, I love you. Lord, help our
marriage. Please change us both. In Jesus' name. Amen.*

July 14

*Hello, my Father. We are camping again in Coronado. Thank you
for the beachfront spot. It was a beautiful day here. Today we saw
a sand shark. I believe that's what you call them. Someone caught
it on their fishing pole. The kids held it. My husband and the boys
rode body boards. It was too cold for me to go in the water. The
kids fed the birds fish crackers. They would throw them up into
the air, and the birds would catch them. My middle guy lost his
boat and asked me, "Mom, will you ask God to find my boat?" So
I prayed, "Jesus, please help me find my son's boat." I was
walking along the beach looking for it when I stubbed my toe on
something, I looked closer and saw it was my son's boat covered
in sand. Lord, you are so faithful at answering prayers.*

*Please help my husband and me to fall in love again, even deeper
than when we were first married. In Jesus' name I pray.*

These journal entries represent such faithfulness of the Lord to me.
When I wrote letters to Jesus, I felt the Lord's presence. I think of brother
Yun, from the book *The Heavenly Man,* who wrote, "I didn't suffer for
Jesus in prison. No! I was with Jesus and I experienced his very real
presence, joy, and peace every day. It's not those in prison for the sake of
the gospel who suffer. The person who suffers is he who never
experiences God's intimate presence."[1] I know that what I went through
wasn't anything near what our imprisoned brothers and sisters have gone
through. Yet I know (and have totally experienced) that Jesus is willing
to be closest to us in our darkest times. Although this was a rough time
for me, wearing myself out trying to get my husband to love me, I
remember it as a sweet time with the Lord. It says in Matthew 11:28,
"Then Jesus said, 'Come to me, all of you who are weary and carry
heavy burdens, and I will give you rest.'" I was weary, and the burden of

trying to make someone love and appreciate me was heavy. God's Word was a healing balm on my bruised, hurting heart.

My husband's love, affection, and kindness were very conditional, but God's wasn't. Romans 8:39 says, "And I am convinced that nothing can ever separate us from God's love. Neither death nor life, neither angels or demons, neither our fears for today nor our worries about tomorrow—not even the powers of hell can separate us from God's love." That was so different from my husband's love. I could be separated from his love over a "wrongly" packed diaper bag or wanting to keep sex just between us.

This was a year that broke me, but praise God, he didn't leave me there. The process was not overnight, but he was beginning to make me a stronger woman in *him*. He would also begin teaching me that we serve a God of boundaries, not because he is mean but because he loves us. You can't get wine without crushing grapes.

10

LET'S TALK BOUNDARIES

"Fearing people is a dangerous trap, but trusting the Lord means safety."

PROVERBS 29:25

DESPERATE PEOPLE RARELY MAKE HEALTHY, godly decisions. I happen to know this from experience. My desperation led to an ungodly compromise and an emotional breakdown.

Whenever my husband would get angry, I would go to prayer and ask God to show me what I had done wrong. How could I have handled it differently so he would not have responded in anger? I would resolve that I just needed to pray more. I thought I was just trying to be a godly submissive wife. But God revealed to me I wasn't submitting out of love of God, but out of fear of a man, my husband. I felt the Lord was saying to me, "Stop trying to put a Christian spin on this. The truth is you are afraid of your husband and of confrontation. You are not to fear any man, not even your husband."

Once again, I was not in fear for my physical safety. Please seek professional help of a trained counselor, or call a domestic violence hotline in your area if you are in danger. Please do not be scared to reach out for help. You should not attempt to go through this alone.

I would always cave to my husband's requests and compromise standards because I feared him. Making decisions based on fear is a trap set by the enemy of our souls. I started to see this recurring theme when I would open my Bible. The passage that convicted me the most was in Luke 12:4–5: "Dear friends, don't be afraid of those who want to kill your body; they cannot do any more to you after that. But I'll tell you whom to fear. Fear God, who has the power to kill you and then throw you into hell. Yes, he's the one to fear."

The only one I was allowed to fear was the Lord. Time and time again I would see in the Word where people did not want to stand for Jesus because it could cost them the approval of man or get them thrown out of the synagogue (in today's terms, church).[1] Or in my case, thrown out of the house.

The Lord was convicting me to stop fearing man and trust *him*. I remember when my husband worked at a NASCAR race, and how so many barely clothed women would always want their picture taken with the firefighters. Being replaced by another is a fear that goes back to the beginning of time. A woman's fear of being replaced by another woman. But God was releasing me of this fear as well.

My security had to come from being a child of God. I could no longer justify allowing my fear to rule me. Isaiah 51:12–15 says it beautifully:

I, yes I, am the one who comforts you. So why are you afraid of mere humans, who wither like the grass and disappear? Yet you have forgotten the Lord, your Creator, the one who stretched out the sky like a canopy and laid the foundations of the earth. Will you remain in constant dread of human oppressors? Will you continue to fear the anger of your enemies? Where is their fury and anger now? It is gone! Soon all you captives will be released! Imprisonment, starvation, and death will not be your fate! For I am the Lord your God, who stirs up the sea, causing its waves to roar. My name is the Lord of Heaven's Armies.

God was and is my provider, not man. God is your provider as well! Not only had the Word encouraged and convicted me not to fear man, but it also demonstrated to me that we serve a God of healthy boundaries.

~

Early in my Christian walk, I was mentored into thinking that truly godly wives *never* confront bad behavior. But after spending time in the whole Word of God, I no longer saw that.

God was calling me to stop enabling such ungodly behavior not only in the bedroom but even when Scott would try to "keep me in line" with his temper or put me in emotional isolation. Through Bible stories of confrontation, I learned it was OK to set up healthy boundaries in my marriage.

One of the first examples from Scripture I would like to share with you is about David, who is referred to as "a man after God's own heart." (1 Samuel 13:14; Acts 13:22) David was not only known by that title but also as a brave and mighty warrior. He also showed another quality during his earlier years that isn't talked about very often; he had the ability to enact healthy boundaries. He unfortunately didn't carry this quality to all his relationships, but we will save those not-so-awesome stories for another time. Like David, many of us sometimes start out with clear godly wisdom in our life one moment and then become clouded with too much praise or prosperity. We can nail it (healthy, godly life choices) one minute followed by an epic nosedive the next. Stay humble and dependent. Let's focus on one of David's "nailed it!" moments.

If you are not familiar with this story, please take the time to read 1 Samuel 24. Saul was the current king, even though the prophet Samuel had anointed David to be the new king. David was waiting for God's timing to make the transfer of power. King Saul was intimidated by David and wanted nothing to do with giving up *any* of his power. His solution was to kill David, regardless of how righteous and loyal David was to him.

Saul was completely blinded by his need for control and power. So that made David his biggest enemy. There was just no convincing Saul otherwise, but that didn't stop David from trying. And that is where we pick up the story. Saul was on his way to find and kill David when nature called. He picked a cave where David and his men were hiding. Saul wasn't aware he wasn't the only one in that cave. David's men tried to convince him to kill Saul, but he refused. Instead, David cut a piece of Saul's robe off to prove to Saul he did not want to harm him.

After Saul left, David yelled out to him and showed him the evidence he could have killed him right there but didn't. Saul responded,

> "Is that really you, my son David?" Then he began to cry. And he said to David, "You are a better man than I am, for you have repaid me good for evil. Yes, you have been amazingly kind to me today, for when the Lord put me in a place where you could have killed me, you didn't do it." (1 Samuel 24:16–18)

There are three things that stand out in this story:

1. David was a man who trusted God to deliver him from a man's evil intentions.
2. Saul with tears gave an awesome repentant "I've seen the light" speech.
3. David said, "That was an awesome speech. I still promise to not harm you, but I still don't trust you until you back it with action."

OK, that is my version of the interaction, but what we do see from David's actions is he still didn't trust Saul enough to follow him back to his place. He decided to keep a safe distance.

Please notice how points 1 and 3 coincide. Keeping yourself safe does not mean you are not trusting God. There are few people in God's Word who showed such bravery when facing an enemy as David did. Coward would not be a word used to describe him. Yet he decided to remain a safe distance until Saul's actions could be tested.

It was a good thing David did, because in 1 Samuel 26, we see Saul really hadn't changed at all. Once again David had an opportunity to kill

Saul but didn't. Instead, David took a spear that was by Saul's head while he was sleeping. When Saul awakened and realized what had happened, we get to hear once again a false repentance. "Then Saul confessed, 'I have sinned. Come back home, my son, and I will no longer try to harm you, for you valued my life today. I have been a fool and very, very wrong.'" (v. 21) Not only did David *not* follow his king home that day, he had one of Saul's young men come and retrieve his spear. David did not even allow his abuser close enough to injure him after his false repentance speech.

David still showed respect for Saul's position as king but also protected himself from his abuser. David's friends encouraged him to seek revenge and strike Saul, but David refused. However, just because he respected Saul's position, he wasn't going to leave himself in a position to be injured so easily.

No matter how respectful David was to Saul and tried to convince him he had no intentions of bringing any harm to him or his position, Saul's mind had become so deceived that he couldn't see David's loyalty and integrity to God and himself. Sometimes it is the same when dealing with an angry or addicted person. They can become convinced you are against them no matter how hard you try to prove otherwise. As they say in Pure Desire, "We believe behavior, not words."[2]

Unfortunately, sometimes in Christian counseling settings, the wife is encouraged or pressured to immediately take back her abusing or addicted spouse before his repentance can be proven by action. If she doesn't, she can sometimes be labeled as rebellious or unforgiving and told to go back and submit to ungodly authority. And yet we see the one given the prestigious title as "a man after God's own heart" refusing to submit to Saul's request.

Hebrews shares with us how we should all have a fear of deliberate continual sin because it can lead to the death of relationships. "Dear friends, if we deliberately continue sinning after we have received the knowledge of the truth, there is no longer any sacrifice that will cover these sins." (Hebrews 10:26) Refusing to give an abusive person access to you doesn't mean you are not trusting God; it means you're not enabling their sin. It did not mean that for King David, and it does not mean that for you. Saul never did come to true godly repentance, so we do not see David having a relationship or any other conversation with Saul.

We will be forever grateful and feel spoiled by the Lord that the pastors in my life at the time knew about the importance of healthy boundaries. Granted, my husband wasn't thanking me in the moment, but *many* times since then he has thanked me and encouraged other women (in my presence, of course) that tough boundaries transformed his life, and they weren't doing their husband any favors by enabling ungodly behavior.

But let's look at another example of God using boundaries.

In Amos 4, we see the Lord is big on boundaries and life consequences.

> "I brought hunger to every city and famine to every town. But still you would not return to me," says the Lord. "I kept the rain from falling when your crops needed it the most. I sent rain on one town but withheld it from another. Rain fell on one field, while another field withered away. People staggered from town to town looking for water, but there was never enough. But still you would not return to me," says the Lord. (vv. 6–8)

He stated his motivation after each set of consequences: "But still you would not return to me." The Lord increased their discomfort, all in hopes of getting them to return to him. I can't think of any example in the Bible where a people group who strayed from serving the Lord returned their hearts to him because he blessed them with more safety and prosperity. I do see throughout the Old Testament that the Lord promised blessing in his children's lives as long as they chose to remain faithful to him. And just like many kings in the Old Testament, we have free will and can have stubborn hearts and we can still choose our own ways. The Lord closed out the chapter in Amos with the consequences of

Israel straying: "Prepare to meet your God in judgment, you people of Israel." (v. 12) The end.

That really stuck with me. The Lord, with all his resources, has boundaries as our best hope in getting our hearts to change. Never once implemented out of revenge but in hopes of bringing life transformation that leads to a prosperous life in Christ.

Just in case you are thinking, "That is the Old Testament God. He has lightened up since Jesus came on scene. We now live under the grace, love, and hugs of the Jesus era." Have you read Revelation? Jesus has not mellowed out.

When studying the life of Jesus, we see him retreating from the needs of the people to go spend time alone with his Father. Jesus did not minister to *every* need that every person had. That is a boundary he set with people. How much more with us, not being Jesus, we should put the same boundary in our lives. (see Luke 5:16 and Mark 1:35) I learned it is OK to say no to people, even family members. (Confession: still not always easy for me. Two things that always seem to resurrect faster than Lazarus from his tomb are pride and people pleasing. May the Good Lord help me!)

We also see an encounter with Jesus healing a man, but this one shows a different interaction than most of the other healings we read about.

As Jesus was returning to Jerusalem, he passed by the Pool of Bethesda where he met a lame man who had been sick for thirty-eight years. "When Jesus saw him and knew he had been ill for a long time, he asked him, "Would you like to get well?." (John 5:6)

Notice Jesus didn't assume the man wanted to get well. Because if you don't even have the "want to," you're not ready for deliverance. As crazy as this sounds, some people prefer their sickness over health. I love how my counselor friend once said, "Never work harder for someone's emotional health than they are willing to work for it themselves." The man had to play a part by believing Jesus could give him the power to do what he had never been able to do before. He listened to what Jesus told him, believed with Jesus by his side it would be different, and he did just that—picked up his mat and walked.

"But afterward Jesus found him in the Temple and told him, 'Now you are well; so stop sinning, or something even worse may happen to you.'" (John 5:14) Jesus, the epitome of love and grace, didn't pull any punches but got straight to the point. He didn't tell the man sinning was no big deal, just do the best he could. He told him if he didn't change his ways, life would end badly for him. Jesus didn't bluff. There are consequences for your life choices.

Even the woman caught in adultery was shown grace within a boundary of "Go and sin no more." (John 8:11) You cannot continue in sinful ways and think you will remain under blessing.

In Matthew 18:3, Jesus spoke very strongly to his disciples right after they asked him who among them would be the greatest: "I tell you the truth (he wants you to know he is not lying or messing around here) **unless you turn from your sins** and become like little children, **you will never** get into the Kingdom of Heaven" (additions and emphasis mine).

And here comes one of the most shocking statements of Jesus, especially if you only see him as the cuddly all-grace Savior: "But if you cause one of these little ones who trusts in me to fall into sin, it would be better for you to have a large millstone tied around your neck and be drowned in the depths of the sea." (Matthew 18:6)

Did Jesus really just say that and connect it with, "I tell you the truth"? That puts a holy fear in me! How I parent matters. It makes me think . . . how am I modeling Jesus to my children, my daughter? Am I modeling a desperation that I will agree to anything just to keep a man from leaving or disapproving of me?

I don't mean to be a downer here, but the verses don't get any cheerier just yet.

"What sorrow awaits the world, because it tempts people to sin. Temptations are inevitable, but what sorrow awaits the person who does the tempting." (Matthew 18:7)

After I read this passage, I realized I was not helping my husband's temptations when I caved to his ungodly desires. I was not living up to my call of being his helpmate. (see Genesis 2:18)

For example, when a husband asks a wife to dress inappropriately sexy in public, it will feed the flames of sexual addiction. According to Scott, one of the reasons a husband wants her to dress like that is to show her off to other men. I am not talking about dressing pretty or cute for your husband or yourself. Enjoy fashion if that is your thing. Without getting descriptive, my husband used to ask me to wear all kinds of inappropriate things in public. I so wanted to be pleasing to him (even more than to God).

Jesus's strong words continue in verses 8–9:

So if your hand or foot causes you to sin, cut it off and throw it away. It's better to enter eternal life with only one hand or one foot than to be thrown into eternal fire with both of your hands and feet. And if your eye causes you to sin, gouge it out and throw it away. It's better to enter life with only one eye than to have two eyes and be thrown into the fire of hell.

Now before you start thinking, "Wow, Anna is just anti-sex. Either that or she thinks God is." I would like to adamantly say "No way!" to both sentiments. I personally *love* sex with my husband. Thank God for the opportunity. I am grateful to be able to share with you that God is even more pro-sex than me. It was his idea, his invention. But as we have been discussing, God is a God of boundaries.

Drink water from your own well—share your love only with your wife. Why spill the water of your springs in the streets, having sex with just anyone? You should reserve it for yourselves. Never share it with strangers. For the Lord sees clearly what a man does, examining every path he takes. An evil man is held captive by his own sins; they are ropes that catch and hold him. He will die for lack of self-control; he will be lost because of his great foolishness. (Proverbs 5:15–17, 21–23)

I loved and still do love my husband. I do not want to aid in my husband's dying for lack of self-control or being lost for all of eternity.

Even though Jesus gives us stern warnings in Matthew 18, let's end with some great encouragement he gives in verses 12–14:

> If a man has a hundred sheep and one of them wanders away, what will he do? Won't he leave the ninety-nine others on the hills and go out to search for the one that is lost? And if he finds it, I tell you the truth he will rejoice over it more than over the ninety-nine that didn't wander away! In the same way, it is not my heavenly Father's will that even one of these little ones should perish.

Our heavenly Father loves you and me and even wandering husbands! He is on the lookout for ways to bring them back home.

As I continued my search in the New Testament, I found that Paul was pro-boundaries with people on several occasions. In 1 Timothy, Paul wrote the most beautiful letter concerning God's amazing mercy and grace for sinners.

> This is a trustworthy saying, and everyone should accept it: "Christ Jesus came into the world to save sinners"—and I am the worst of them all. But God had mercy on me so that Christ Jesus could use me as a prime example of his great patience with even the worst sinners. Then others will realize that they, too, can believe in him and receive eternal life. (1 Timothy 1:15–16)

But right after that rich and deep description of the grace and mercy of God, we see Paul kick off his instructions by sharing how there are some people who are *not* in need of more grace, but instead, some tough love to turn from their wicked behavior.

Timothy, my son, here are my instructions for you, based on the
prophetic words spoken about you earlier. May they help you
fight well in the Lord's battles. Cling to your faith in Christ, and
keep your conscience clear. For some people have deliberately
violated their consciences; as a result, their faith has been
shipwrecked. Hymenaeus and Alexander are two examples. I
threw them out and handed them over to Satan so they might
learn not to blaspheme God. (1 Timothy 1:18–20)

By giving in to my husband, I was "violating my conscience" in
hopes of keeping my husband's approval. Yet this passage also shows us
that for those who continued to violate their consciences (continuing to
walk in sin), their faith was shipwrecked. Paul's solution? Not more
grace but hand them over to Satan to learn that was not the life they
desired. The thought of being handed over to Satan would make me
tremble. I don't want anything, especially my corrupt desires, to remove
me from the Lord's safekeeping.

In another letter written by Paul, healthy boundaries are still the best
hope in turning hearts back around. "I can hardly believe the report about
the sexual immorality going on among you—something that even pagans
don't do." (1 Corinthians 5:1a) Paul continued to speak to a specific case
in the church concerning a man's continuous sexual sin and how they
should respond to him. "Then you must throw this man out and hand him
over to Satan so that his sinful nature will be destroyed and he himself
will be saved on the day the Lord returns." (v. 5) Please note the motive
again is not revenge but love in hopes of making his life right with God.

When I wrote to you before, I told you not to associate with
people who indulge in sexual sin. But I wasn't talking about
unbelievers who indulge in sexual sin, or are greedy, or cheat
people, or worship idols. You would have to leave this world to
avoid people like that. I meant that you are not to associate
with anyone who claims to be a believer yet indulges in sexual
sin, or is greedy, or worships idols, or is abusive, or is a
drunkard, or cheats people. Don't even eat with such people. It

isn't my responsibility to judge outsiders, but it certainly is your responsibility to judge those inside the church who are sinning. God will judge those on the outside; but as the Scriptures say, "You must remove the evil person from among you." (vv. 9–13)

Wow! It appears God does expect there to be boundaries in our relationships. Some might say that passage was not meant for spouses. I do not see that exception written there. If God takes sexual sin and abusiveness that seriously to say to throw the offender out and hand him over to Satan, so should we. To me that does sound harsh, and to think that is in the "gentle Jesus" section of the Bible! But we see it is motivated by love, in hopes of gaining true repentance that leads to salvation. (1 Corinthians 5:5)

Now before some of my wounded women friends start thinking, "Yeah, let's get them!" and start searching the internet for the best deal on pitchforks and torches, with add-on items of tar and feathers, please allow me to share some caution.

The Bible also has a lot to say about the person bringing correction to another and what that confrontation should look like. God's Word says a lot about gentleness and humility. During my journey with my husband, I came across the story of the parable of the pharisee and the tax collector during prayer time one evening. In this story, the pharisee is busy reminding God of what an awesome follower he is, giving God an itemized list of all his good deeds. Meanwhile the tax collector, with humility, realizes what a sinner he is and stands far back beating his chest, asking for God's mercy. Jesus ended the story with, "For those who exalt themselves will be humbled, and those who humble themselves will be exalted." (Luke 18:14b)

In that moment the Lord spoke to me, "Your husband knows what he is. You don't realize what you are." I thought I was better than my husband. I was the pharisee in this story. And in true pharisee fashion, I started to defend my position with, "Well, of course I think I am better than him! It's hard not to think you're not better than someone who tears apart a house and breaks things. Look at how he treats me! I don't treat people like that! It seems like he doesn't even care about honoring your Word. I do! How can I not think of myself as better than him?"

Yep. I seriously said those things to the Lord (#embarrassed).

When I focused on how the story ended, that's when I went facedown and asked for God's forgiveness and mercy for my arrogance. "Thank you, Lord. You are faithful to forgive!" The Word says in James 4:6, "And he gives grace generously. As the Scriptures say, 'God opposes the proud but gives grace to the humble.'"

God uses boundaries to help a person arrive at true repentance. But they should be established with love and humility.

What about when we are in physical danger? Sometimes as believers we can become out of balance with viewing things from only a spiritual side. There are times when we must rely on protective laws set in place by our system of justice. Paul was not afraid to take full advantage of his rights as a Roman citizen.

We read in Acts 22:25, "When they tied Paul down to lash him, Paul said to the officer standing there, 'Is it legal for you to whip a Roman citizen who hasn't even been tried?'"

Paul was letting those men know he had rights under the law as a Roman citizen. "The soldiers who were about to interrogate Paul quickly withdrew when they heard he was a Roman citizen, and the commander was frightened because he had ordered him bound and whipped." (v. 29) Using the law or court system to protect you or your children does not mean you are not trusting God. If you are in a dangerous situation, please don't hesitate to protect yourself and family.

In Acts 12, we see God made a way for Peter to escape prison and Peter took it. According to the authorities, he was supposed to stay in prison but followed God's guidance instead. In Acts 16, we read how Paul also had his chains fall off and prison doors open but chose to stay. Just because God provided an opportunity to leave, he did not take it. He felt the Lord had purpose in him staying. One decision was not holier than the other. You must seek God's will on whether to stay or leave, not out of fear of what your spouse will say or do. Not out of fear of what people might say or do. It is not of God to make decisions out of fear. Stay because you have heard from God. Go because you believe that is what God is telling you to do in your situation. Seek God daily. But if you have children in the house, your priority is always their emotional and physical safety. Please do not doubt that.

In my personal experience, God asked me to stay for a season to show unconditional love. As stated before, true love isn't afraid to put up boundaries. I had to trust the Lord with my husband and be willing to leave him if he did not want to honor God with his actions and life choices.

As I felt called to set boundaries with my husband, I would always ask the Lord to confirm it in his Word. As I read from the One Year Bible year after year, I continually saw a recurring theme of amazing grace and love, partnered with boundaries for our good. Because God loves us so much, he will put up boundaries in our lives. I was learning that true love is willing to be uncomfortable and risk not being liked or loved in return.

When placing a boundary, always ask the Lord to reveal the motive driving your decision. Proverbs 16:2 says, "People may be pure in their own eyes, but the Lord examines their motives." Pray and ask God to reveal your true motives. Are they to help bring healing or hurt to the other person?

God asks us to love him more than life itself. It means more than in just a Christian martyr kind of way. Will we be willing to lose our comfortable life, including the dreams we've had, to honor and serve Jesus? When we live in fear of our spouses—whether it be physically, emotionally, or in fear of being abandoned—and we compromise Jesus's standard just so we can keep these things in our lives, are we creating idols? (See Deuteronomy 4:16.)

I think it comes down to whom we're trying to please. In Galatians 1:10, Paul described his motivations: "Obviously, I'm not trying to win the approval of people, but of God. If pleasing people were my goal, I would not be Christ's servant."

Our life struggles are difficult and many, but we have the trustworthy Word of God Almighty, our loving heavenly Father to guide us through our personal "valley of the shadow of death." (Psalm 23:4) The tools that our Father has given us are both spiritual and practical, so please don't ignore either one. Relational boundaries are used by our heavenly Father over and over again with us, and he is the best at relationships. So do not be afraid of putting them in place in your life as well. Fear not, for he is with us and will never abandon you or me. You must be courageous!

Be patient with the Lord, your spouse, and yourself. Remember, great is his faithfulness. You are not alone. "Taste and see that the Lord is good. Oh, the joys of those who take refuge in him!" (Psalm 34:8)

11

DISCOVERY

ALTHOUGH SOME THINGS got better after our getaway, Scott and I still had a long way to go. Google hadn't been around for that long. It was all new. Today, it seems simple and obvious to know you could check someone's browsing history. Unfortunately, now they have private browsers and all sorts of ways to hide one's activity on the internet. I don't remember exactly how I accidentally found a little box that had all sorts of graphic descriptions.

However, I vividly remember the feeling of panic, my heart starting to race as I continued to read titles searched for. Sick to my stomach, having a hard time believing what I was seeing. Thinking there must be a mistake. *Just calm down. There has to be an explanation.* I didn't know what to do. I had been listening to Dr. Dobson on the radio every morning, and I knew he had family counselors. So I called them. They sent me a free book, *Living with Your Husband's Secret Wars* by Marsha Means, because I told them I didn't want my husband to see a purchase on the credit card and ask me what I had purchased. (I will be forever grateful for that ministry's kindness.)

I also learned about an internet-monitoring program called Covenant Eyes. I called them, and a kind, helpful man talked me through how to look up history and some other things. I will be eternally thankful for the compassion and patience that anonymous man had with me that day. I just remember asking over and over again, "You mean, he for sure typed those words in the computer and searched that?" He gently confirmed what I feared.

Thankfully, my husband had been scheduled for overtime, so I had the space I needed to get my bearings. The next day, when Scott was on his way home from work, he asked if I wanted to meet him for dinner. Refusing to go out for dinner never happens, and I didn't want to tip him off until I knew what the right thing to do was. I was unusually quiet during dinner. When he asked why, I dismissed it as just being tired from the kids and him working a lot. I didn't want to tell him in the restaurant. I was too afraid the dam of tears would give way and flood out the whole restaurant.

I made it out to the parking lot before he asked if everything was OK. I started to cry. I quietly muttered, "I happened to see your extra activities you have been into on the internet." He instantly hugged me and reassured me that it wasn't him, that the computer would just suggest those things. He never typed those things in. He looked me right into my eyes, so gently, with so much concern . . . and lied to me.

I started to believe him. He was so convincing. Even with evidence, I started to doubt the truth because the truth was too scary to face.

We went home. I still wasn't sure what to do, so I started reading the book the ministry sent me. I thought maybe I could just forget what happened, and we could go back to living as we were—best friends who loved laughing together with our kids and doing church ministry. But of course, cancer never gets better left untreated; it only grows worse until it spreads to the point of death.

One night when we were being intimate, my husband brought me over to the computer to show me something he wanted to watch while we were together. I didn't have the guts to stop it. I didn't want him to be mad at me. Afterward, I felt horrible. I felt like I had failed God in holding the boundary. So I told my husband, "I don't ever want to do that again. Not because I'm prudish, just the opposite. I know what I am capable of without the Lord's protection over my mind. I want to honor God in every area of our life."

Scott got very angry with me and told me I needed to stop being such a prude. I don't remember everything he said. I tended to blank out when he would yell at me, but I vividly remember him saying, "I am so sick and tired of you being insecure about this. There is nothing wrong with what we did."

I went to go sleep on the couch. I couldn't believe he was actually defending porn! In the middle of the night, I called a friend who was living overseas at the time because her husband was in the military. The Lord had brought this friend into my life a year before and had used her to speak a truth into my life that I needed to hear, so I respected her opinion.

My friend couldn't seem to understand why I was so upset. She told me she believed there was nothing wrong with it, as long as you watch it together. I was in disbelief! When I met her last year, she did not hold that opinion when she caught her husband looking at young, nude teenage girls, but now it was OK as long as you do it together?

I did not see the difference between porn and drugs. Like drugs, you need more and more to give you the same high you seek. So I asked her what the difference was. It was like saying we could do drugs as long as we did them together—as long as we got high together then it was OK. She hung up the phone, never to talk to me again.

I went to the Lord after that conversation, and as usual, he used Scripture to answer my question of whether she was right. The Lord reminded me of the story of Peter, how one minute he answered one of Jesus's questions and Jesus replied, "Way to nail it, Peter! It is God who revealed that to you!" (my translation), but a few verses later Jesus reprimanded Peter: "Get away from me, Satan!" he said. "You are seeing things merely from a human point of view, not from God's." (Mark 8:33b)

It is so important for us to be in the Word of God for ourselves, so that well-intentioned or deceived people don't lead us astray. Whenever I lead a Bible study, I always share with my ladies that Scripture and tell them, "Don't take my word for it. Always test anything I say with the Scriptures." We see that same example set by Paul himself. (see 1 John 4:1)

I felt like I was standing alone. That was just what the enemy wanted me to believe. That's also what the enemy wants *you* to believe. Don't fall for it!

The Word of God and the book sent to me were showing me that I wasn't crazy, I wasn't making too much of this, and I wasn't alone. Many women have had to walk this path. I wasn't without hope. Most importantly, I was learning I didn't have to be a helpless victim without life choices. One phrase I will always remember from *Love Must Be Tough* is the quote Dr. Dobson said: "It is only when he sees everything of value to him—his home, his children, his wife, his reputation—begin to slip away that his choices will become clear. . . . What I'm saying is that an early blowout is better than a slow leak."[1]

Between reading that and the Lord reminding me of his upside-down kingdom Scriptures like Luke 17:33, "If you cling to your life, you will lose it, and if you let your life go, you will save it," God was asking me to trust him completely and be obedient to him, regardless of the cost. The Lord had made it clear to me: it was time to end the slow leak in exchange for the blowout.

Marsha Means gave an example of a letter to write to a spouse who is a sexual addict.[2] I had a friend help me write mine. I would encourage you to do the same if you find yourself in this position. My original letter was about two pages long, filled with so many things I had never spoken of before. But that was not the time to unleash all of my hurt built up from over the years. My friend cut it down to two paragraphs for me to read to Scott. I'm grateful for the letter intervention. Friends are so necessary to help us to stay focused when life overwhelms us.

Means also talked about how you should not confront a sexual addict alone:

Dr. Richard Irons of Golden Valley Health Center says that, "individually confronting addicts is like playing one-on-one basketball against Michael Jordan. We won't win. They are too skilled at denial and delusion. . . . [W]hen we take a team of people, even if none of them are NBA caliber, the team will probably get the job done."[3]

This one paragraph played a big role in my willingness to have someone with me when I confronted Scott. I knew I wasn't betraying his trust by having someone there. The Lord provided me with two dear friends to come with me.

I also needed to prepare myself for the confrontation. As important as the words of my letter were, there was another thing of equal importance—the delivery. Dr. Dobson put it like this:

> The Precipitated crisis, first, must be accompanied by an entire change of attitude. Instead of begging, pleading, wringing of your hands, and whimpering like an abused puppy, you, as the vulnerable partner, must appear strangely calm and assured. The key word is confidence, and it is of maximum importance. Your manner should say, "I believe in me. I'm no longer afraid. I can cope, regardless of the outcome. I know something I'm not talking about. I've had my day of sorrow, and I'm through crying. God and I can handle whatever life puts in the path."[4]

So, with a letter in my hand and a trust in the Lord to get me through, two of my friends waited with me for my husband to arrive home. I had our kids at my parents' house, so they would be protected from the unexpected. When Scott pulled into the driveway, I met him at his vehicle and told him we needed to talk. We went inside and as planned, I read a letter that went something like this.

*Scott, I am here to let you know I can longer participate in or tolerate the porn use in this house. Not because I am insecure or a prude but because I have decided to honor Jesus above all else. Even if that means I have to do it alone. I cannot make you desire to do the same. The Lord has shown me I can only control my choices. I am not going to continue to try and convince you that it is **not** OK. God's Word clearly states if you even look at a woman lustfully, you have committed adultery.*

*I love you and our children love you. I hope you choose to stay
married to us, but the only way that can happen is if you get help.
I have already scheduled a counseling appointment this Tuesday
with Pastor _______. I will be there regardless of your decision. I
need help in how to deal with this in a godly way. I hope you will
decide to join me in the process. If you choose not to, I am
available on Wednesday, when we can meet to discuss how to best
handle our separation. I am going to leave now, but our two
friends are here today because they love you and want to help
and support you anyway they can. I do love you, Scott, and I am
praying for you.*

After I finished reading, I walked out of the house. My friends stayed
behind to help encourage him. It was best I not stay there and get sucked
into a conversation that would be unhealthy. If Scott desired that
conversation, it would take place with a pastor who understood addiction
or with a counselor. I drove to another friend's house, and right after
crossing the threshold of her front door, I collapsed onto the floor into a
heap of sobs. I had looked very calm and composed, just like the two
books recommended, while reading the letter, but I couldn't hold it in
any longer. Sobs turned into prayers before the Lord in that entryway of
my friend's house. I called out to God to please save my family.

Before reading the letter to my husband, I had asked my friends to
help me be strong. I told my girlfriends, "I know me. I will come out of
the gates strong, but if he doesn't come for me, don't let me give in."

Don't make a boundary you're not willing to hold to. I had no idea if
Scott would choose me; I just knew there was no going back. I believed
the Lord was clear, and I had to trust him even if it meant going at life as
a single momma. I love my friends; they gave me their word to help me
stay strong. I had many other friends interceding for our family. I will be
forever grateful and unable to repay that debt. I can only pay it forward
and pray for other women's families. I waited at my friend's house to
receive an update of how it went.

They said my husband didn't say much, but he knew what he was
doing was wrong and didn't want to lose his family. They prayed with

him. I went to my parents' house to spend the night there. My younger two were in bed, asleep, but my oldest was still awake. I would always joke that my oldest could move in with my parents and never miss me. My parents lived on five acres of non-stop boyhood fun. They had four-wheelers to drive through dirt and mud, and trees to climb.

My son had never asked to come home from Grandma and Grandpa's house, except for this night. There was nothing in the natural that would have tipped my kids off that we were having troubles. I made sure to act as normal as possible. I will never forget the look on my son's face when he rolled over in bed as I walked into the room. He looked at me and said, "Mom, I want to go home."

"We can't go home tonight. It is getting late." I tried to sound upbeat and told him, "Besides, tonight is going to be a fun night. I am even going to spend the night here with you!"

He looked at me and said, "Tonight is not a fun night. It is an evil night!" I quickly stepped out of the room and cried, thinking, *He is right —tonight is an evil night. Satan is trying to tear our family apart. Life decisions are being made tonight.* I gathered myself together and prayed with a friend on the phone and then went and prayed with my son. We went home the next day because I knew my husband would be gone the next couple of days, working shifts.

I had learned from the previous year to take care of my body as well as my spiritual side. I made sure I stayed off sugar and ate even when I didn't feel like it to keep my blood sugar stable. I interceded for my family passionately once I got the kids into bed, followed by watching a good comedy before I went to bed. In 2001, I would stay up around the clock, pacing the floors and praying. I wasn't going to fall for the schemes of the enemy this time, thinking God needed me awake, keeping an eye on my problems. I would leave them in the Lord's capable hands. I invested my time in prayer, then trusted the Lord to do his work. "The Lord himself will fight for you. Just stay calm." (Exodus 14:14) "Be still, and know that I am God!" (Psalm 46:10a)

Thankfully, Scott decided to meet with the pastor. As grateful as I was for him wanting to keep our marriage, I implored him, "Please don't stay for me and the kids if porn is what you really want. Please think about it because I don't want to be seen as your prison warden. A relationship can never make it under that pretense." I told him I wouldn't go through another year like the 9/11 year, where he was going to try and punish me for wanting to honor God. "I'm not compromising anymore in this area. Not only porn, but all the fantasy scenarios that involve other people. If it can't be just us in this marriage, then there is no marriage."

Gary Thomas, a writer known for his high value of marriage, provided great advice in an article addressing porn use.

> If your husband is unrepentantly engaging in porn use, you don't have to "share" him with a website. If he's returning from a bachelor party that stopped off at a strip club, you needn't feel like it's your "wifely" duty to be an "outlet" for lust that was generated miles away. You can say, "I want to have a fantastic sexual relationship with you, even one that will wear you out, but I won't share you. Once it's clear that you're dealing with this other issue, we can begin rebuilding our sexual relationship. But I will never share you. You've broken our trust, you've dishonored our marriage, and now we have to put the relationship back together before we can be sexually intimate."[5]

Before receiving the resources from Focus on the Family, I came close to compromising. I had made a counseling appointment at a secular place through our medical insurance. I told the counselor that I had found my husband was going to porn sites. I told her it went against our faith, and I didn't feel good about participating in that, but now he wouldn't even talk to me. I shared with the counselor if he would talk to me, maybe we could come to a compromise—come to an agreement on how much was OK.

Yep, that's what I said. A bit embarrassing to read now. That's just like the devil, to make me think sin *management* instead of sin *deliverance* is a great option.

I have sat across the table from women, hearing how they agreed to let another woman into their bed with her and her husband because her husband's fantasy was to have a "three way." And with tears and devastation written all over their faces, how horrible it was to watch and take part in—all in hopes of keeping their husband's love. Oh, that we would see our value in the Lord's eyes and refuse to compromise. It never leads to deliverance. "Don't you realize that this sin is like a little yeast that spreads through the whole batch of dough?" (1 Corinthians 5:6b)

Praise God my husband wouldn't talk to me right away after he told me he was tired of me being insecure about having porn in our marriage! It gave God time to help me come to my senses and to get resources into my hands to rid my faulty, ungodly thinking! The problem with sin management versus deliverance is sin refuses to be managed. It may play nice for a short season, just long enough to get you comfortable, before it brings death to all you value.

"Don't you realize that you become the slave of whatever you choose to obey? You can be **a slave to sin, which leads to death**, or you can choose to obey God, which leads to righteous living." (Romans 6:16, emphasis mine)

Before God brought freedom to Scott's life, I felt like we were caught in this cycle of good and bad seasons, steadfastness and compromises. Holding the boundaries was the only time I saw us moving toward freedom. But before that was achieved, we had to walk through some blame-shifting days. But God was with me, helping me to see the truth. Like this conversation.

Scott: "I wouldn't get so angry if you wouldn't ________." I can't actually remember what he threw in that blank, but he had said that sentence with many different fill-in-the-blanks throughout our marriage.

Me: "I'm sorry, I cannot accept that. Because the truth is just like the Lord showed me. Like when I use to blame you for my anxiety attacks, but it wasn't your fault for my anxiety. I felt very justified. Who wouldn't have panic attacks living here never knowing when you would get angry? But God delivered me from that because the truth is, I had anxiety attacks long before there was Scott in my life. And the truth is, you have had a temper problem long before I was in your life. I have tried for years to fulfill all your requests in hopes that you would stop getting angry with me, and it doesn't work. So I no longer accept it as my fault or responsibility. Just like you are not responsible for my peace or lack of it."

It would be impossible for a book to tell you how you should handle each situation, or how boundaries look on a day-to-day basis. For me, I had to be in daily prayer and asking and believing James 1:5: "If you need wisdom, ask our generous God, and he will give it to you. He will not rebuke you for asking." So along with prayer, I would seek counsel from older, godly women.[6]

I can remember one situation, not long after the porn confrontation, Scott started watching a new sitcom that was all about the main character hooking up with women. There really was no other plot line, and it was filled with one crude joke after another. It aired when we usually went to bed. So while lying in bed one night, I just started praying, "Lord, I don't know what to do in this situation."

Just as much as enabling brings death to a marriage, so does trying to control another person. The Lord reminded me that I can only control me and what I watch. There are things that aren't exactly porn but definitely not edifying. I said, "You know, honey, I just don't really care for this show, so you go ahead and watch it, but I think I'm just going to go into the other room and read for a while and come back later." Because of the Lord's help, I was able to convey it in a loving tone and tried to prepare myself for him not to change the channel. But that isn't what happened at all.

My husband quickly grabbed the remote and said, "Oh, that's OK, honey, we don't have to watch this. Let's put something else on instead." The show was never turned on again. I know I had to be prepared not to be bitter if it had not worked out that way.

Another answered prayer was getting rid of cable. I never mentioned it to my husband, only to the Lord. I was so tired of all the junk that was on TV. Not only the movie channels, but the infomercial that was on every morning of *Girls Gone Wild*. You could not block it out because it was technically an infomercial. They gave it the same TV rating as the weather channel! So when my kids would channel surf for *Madeleine*, or *Blue's Clues*, the next channel would be the *Girls Gone Wild* 30-minute commercial. So I prayed, wishing we could just get rid of cable altogether. Sure enough, not long after that, the satellite company made a mistake on our bill and increased the rate. I remember Scott looking at the bill, getting frustrated, and saying, "I'm so sick of these people always messing up our bill and raising their rates. I just want to cancel TV altogether!"

"OK, honey, I think that sounds like a great idea!"

There were times throughout our marriage the Lord asked me to confront. Other times to just trust and pray. When you should do one and not the other, well, that is where you pray for guidance and seek godly counsel.

Rather than try and address every form of boundary, which I don't think is possible, and describe what each looks like in a variety of everyday situations, I've included just a couple because I believe you must seek the Lord for your own personal situation.

During this time of my life, I would pray Jeremiah 33:3 every day. "Call to me and I will answer you and tell you great and unsearchable things you do not know." (NIV) I reminded the Lord of his promise to help me and tell me "things I do not know," like what to do in this situation! Being as I was a bit overwhelmed during this time of life with my kids being so young and sick all the time, I didn't really take the time to research what was happening in the Word surrounding this verse. I remember hearing it spoken and thinking, "That's exactly what I need in my life!" So I added it to my daily Scripture prayer time. I would make my daily call to the Lord.

Reading the context of it now, I think, *Wow, how applicable to my life it was, and I didn't even know it at the time.* The promise of Jeremiah 33:3 was *not* written during a time of awesome blessing, security, and prosperity. It was told to Jeremiah when he was being held captive. Yet the Lord reminded Jeremiah of who was talking to him—the One who made the heavens and the earth. He proceeded to tell Jeremiah the city would be destroyed due to wickedness. And then comes one of my favorite words: nevertheless. "Nevertheless, the time will come when I will heal Jerusalem's wounds and give it prosperity and true peace." (v. 6) It felt like my house was being destroyed due to wickedness, but God had a "nevertheless" waiting for me. These are some of my journal entries I wrote while I waited for my "true peace" to arrive.

August 14

Hello, sweet Jesus. You have always been so faithful to me. Lord, you are an almighty God. A God of great miracles. I pray all your angels around our house. Lord, soften Scott's heart. Lord, I intercede on his behalf. I pray in the name of Jesus for Satan to get out of our marriage. Send Christian men who live passionate lives for you who can speak into his life. Give him the desire to be accountable and pure. I take every lie and thought captive and cast it out in Jesus' name. Lord, I do not receive the enemy's lies that he tries to speak about our marriage. I do receive the truth from you, Jesus, that you brought us together. Thank you, Lord, for the work you are doing in our lives. As painful as it is, Lord, I pray that any lies or sin in any of our family members would be exposed. I thank you, Jesus. In Jesus' name I pray.

August 17

Today I will ask Scott to leave. I have found that he has been using porn on the internet. I've confronted him, and he shows no remorse. Today I will be strong when I face this situation. I am a child of the King, and He's given all I need to deal with this. Just as David did, I will strengthen myself in the Lord. I will not be weak or be manipulated. I am standing up for righteousness.

August 18

Just as the song says that I listened to right now, I stand in awe of you! Thank you, Jesus! You gave me strength for something I know I had no strength of my own to offer. The very thought of confronting Scott would literally make me vomit. I felt like just a blob on the floor. I just wanted to curl up on the ground and pray you would make me disappear. I think it was Job who prayed he

wished he had never been born. The thought of all my life dreams
. . . I don't want to focus on my fears. I experienced my own shock
and awe last night when my friends came with me to read my
letter. And Jesus, it was all you who gave me the strength to say
what I had to say. Lord, I know we are still at the beginning of
our journey, but I know you have victory for us so long as we are
obedient to your guidance.

August 19

Lord, thank you. Tonight, Scott called from work. It went well. I
just wanted to not go to bed without saying thank you.

August 20

Oh, how faithful you are to speak to me and comfort and guide
me. It is 6:00 a.m. Although Scott and I talked last night, I was in
bed still struggling with anxiety, and I came out here to pray. The
Bible says in 2 Timothy 1:7, "For God has not given us a spirit of
fear and timidity, but of power, love, and self-discipline." When I
went to get my Bible out of the car to look up Scripture, a napkin
fell out of my Bible. It was the verse my friend read after I spoke
and broke down at the mother-daughter banquet. Romans 16:19:
"For the report of your obedience has reached everyone;
therefore I am rejoicing over you, but I want you to be wise in
what is good and innocent in what is evil." (NASB) Oh, my sweet
Jesus, just this second, I looked at the next verse! "The God of
peace will soon crush Satan under your feet." (Romans 16:20,
NASB) Thank you, Jesus. You are almighty and powerful. Praise
be the name of Jesus.

August 22

Hello, my Jesus. Tomorrow we go to our first counseling appt.
I'm not looking forward to it. Lord, I will focus on you and you
will get me through it. Please be in the room with us. Help us to
both hear what we need to. Guide me in what to say. Please give
the pastor wisdom when we meet with him tomorrow. I know

whatever awaits me, you will be there. Lord, help me to be the kind of wife you want me to be. Prepare Scott's and my heart, Lord. Soften them to your will. In Jesus' name I pray.

August 23

Hello, my Jesus. We went to our first counseling appointment. Lord, please give Scott the strength to do what he needs to do. Lord, our marriage is in your hands. Help me and teach me to be the wife he needs me to be. Help him to see me as his friend and someone who wants to help him and love him.

(7:30 p.m.) Oh Jesus, how I need you. I'm feeling discouraged right now. When I look at my situation through my eyes, I get so down. Scott put the Covenant Eyes program on the computer. We blocked some of the TV stations. You remind me that if I knew the outcome, it wouldn't be called faith. The only words that I can say is, save our marriage, Jesus! Only you can change us into the way we should be.

August 24

Hello, my Jesus. I woke up at 5:00 a.m. feeling anxious. Thank you for reminding me the biggest stealer of my peace is me. Worrying about what is in my future or even tomorrow. I remembered reading something at a women's retreat how you are called, "I Am." Right now your name is not "I Will" or "I Was" but "I AM." I know I can make it through right now with you!

September 12

Hello my Jesus. Yesterday they had a lot of shows marking the anniversary of September 11. It was very sad. Hard to believe two years have gone by. I don't know how people in this world make it without you. Today the doctors called, my pap came back irregular. I have to go and have a procedure done to check for precancerous stuff. I had part of my cervix removed already. Lord, I can't help but wish . . . Well, you know what I wish. I know

*it does no good to speak of it. It would just hurt Scott's feelings.
Lord, please help my kids keep themselves pure until their
wedding night. Please keep their future brides and groom pure
for them. It is your way and the safest way to keep from diseases.
My middle guy has now crawled up on me and wants me to hug
him. I will talk with you later. In Jesus' name I pray.*

I found out I had tested positive for HPV, which leads to cervical cancer. It is a sexually transmitted disease (STD). I was too embarrassed to write it at the time in my journal. Many get STDs from when their spouse cheats. It is quite humiliating. I always encourage women to get tested for STDs when their husband has been unfaithful.

October 2

*Hello, Lord. It is 9:30 p.m. Tomorrow I have my biopsy on my
cervix. Lord, please heal that area. Thank you for my family and
for giving me peace with everything. Be with Scott tonight at
work, help him to sleep well, keep him safe, help him to be a good
example of you. In Jesus' name, amen.*

That night, I was so scared about possibly having cervical cancer. My mom had breast cancer when she was just thirty. I started to fear the thought of not being there for my kids. But after reading my One Year Bible, the Lord did what he always does when I need encouragement; he highlighted a Scripture that spoke to me. On this occasion, it was Isaiah 66:9a: "Do I bring to the moment of birth and not give delivery?" That one phrase . . . I felt the Lord asking me, "Anna, have I brought you this far just to leave you? Of course not!"

In that moment, I knew regardless of the test results, the Lord would be with me, and that made it all feel doable. I don't know how the Lord does it, but he has Scripture speak to me—comfort me when I'm scared. It lets me know that the Lord sees and hears me. Reminds me he will never leave me nor forsake me in times of trouble, not now, not ever!

October 17

Hello, my Jesus. I couldn't go to sleep, so I just wanted to take this time to thank you. You are growing me out of my fears. I'm getting so much out of my Bible study. Thank you, Jesus. Your peace is a wonderful thing. I am enjoying my family so much. You daily remind me to hold on to you. You are so amazingly good to us. I love you, Jesus. Please continue to fill me up and exchange my fears for your peace and love.

In Jesus' name, amen. YOU MAKE ME EXCITED TO LIVE!

November 22

Hello, my Jesus. I love you so much. Lately I've been overwhelmed with the call you have put on my life. I can't describe it. I feel it inside, just like Scott knew as a little boy he wanted to be a fireman. I knew I wanted to be a speaker of encouragement to others. Oh, Father, I have been pacing in my bedroom just envisioning the future. I feel like a racehorse just waiting to get out of the gates.

This entry amazed me. Oh, how the Lord works things out. Just the previous week, I was telling a friend I felt like it was time to walk out the call the Lord had given me years ago. I was out of excuses and left only with the decision to be obedient to the call or not. Also, I shared with her how the Lord has always opened doors for me that should not be opened for someone like me. If I had to fill out a résumé for a job, it would be blank because it has been nothing but God's faithfulness that has made any accomplishments possible. The Lord has always provided opportunities and provision for me in ridiculous amounts.

I could have never imagined how he would answer these prayers from many years ago. You could say the Lord Ephesians 3:20'd these prayers! And my dear friend, our future was not looking bright when these were written. Yet I am reminded of Hebrews 11:1: "Faith shows the reality of what we hope for; it is the evidence of things we cannot see."

I would like to say something to my sweet sisters who may be reading this, and your marriage did not make it. You prayed hard and believed big. I mean this with everything in me and believe it to be a biblical truth. *Victory is not defined by a restored marriage but by obedient faith.* We all love what we call success stories. The Bible describes obedience to God as the success story. Was John the Baptist any less successful because he was beheaded in jail, instead of like Peter, who had a miraculous jail escape?

Read Hebrews 11:33–40. It begins with stories the world loves to hear: "By faith these people overthrew kingdoms . . . shut the mouths of lions"—a very long list of those examples. People usually stop right there. They never want to finish the sentence that starts with, "But others were tortured, refusing to turn from God in order to be set free. They placed their hope in a better life after the resurrection." (v. 36) It goes on with a very long list of how many others were tortured, imprisoned, or killed. Some were even being sawed in half. The Word says, "They were too good for this world." (v. 38)

Your marriage may have been "sawed in half." Do not be ashamed to be counted among the "others." The Lord and the crowd of witnesses are cheering for you! They are smiling down, so proud of your refusal of compromise just to make your temporal life more comfortable. There will come a day, when the Lord will wipe away every tear, right all the wrongs. Hold fast, my dear, hold your head high with the lifter of your head![7]

12

MY BOUNDARIES

THE LAST TIME my husband was f—ing me off and yelling at me, we were standing in our bedroom between the computer and our bed. I was trying hard not to smile. Not because I was trying to be antagonizing, I just happened to be having a surreal, out-of-body experience. Perhaps better said, I was having peace. I was trying not to smile while he was yelling at me because on the inside, I was talking to Jesus, my best friend. I was telling him, "You did it, Lord. You did it! Not only am I no longer scared, but I feel I have a one-man party going on in here!"

For the first time, I no longer saw my husband as this big, scary figure. I felt sorry for him, because not having peace is miserable. But just like the Lord showed me that Scott is not the giver of peace in my life, neither am I for him. It took me coming to the end of myself, so tired of being scared, to finally just surrender what I thought I could never give up. And as cheesy and cliché as it sounds, let go and let God. Scott couldn't save me from my lifelong struggle with fear, only God could. I couldn't save or deliver my husband from his anger or lust problem. Only God could do that for him. But just like David waited for God to work in an angry, unstable Saul's life, he trusted God, while also maintaining his safety boundaries. That is what I began to do.

I just stood there, staring at Scott, waiting for him to pause. Not crying, cowering, or even being angry.

Before this "conversation" occurred, I had discovered he had emptied my lingerie drawer and thrown everything out. The nightgowns I was given for my wedding at my bridesmaids' party, all gone. That hurt. More of my special mementos, especially from my wedding, gone forever. This angry outburst all started because I asked if he had been looking at porn on the internet. I wasn't accusing him; I was just checking. I was getting ready to speak at a women's Bible study. I didn't want to be a hypocrite saying we were all great, because I didn't want to project a false image. I wanted reassurance that the image people had of us outside our house matched the inside.

After this happened, I brought my complaint to the Lord. I shared with the Lord how my husband yelling at me was one thing, but I was so tired of him throwing my cherished mementos or even practical items, like our toddlers' shoes, in the trash when I didn't get them picked up.

One time while on the phone with my friend Gina, I was standing in front of my husband's cherished fire trucks, telling her I was going to do it this time. I was going to throw them out, just so he could see what it felt like to lose something he loved. I couldn't do it, not even just one of them. I didn't want to hurt him. I just wished he could see what it felt like so he would stop.

While talking with the Lord, I was reminded of a story I had heard when we were first married from Zig Ziglar's series, *Courtship After Marriage*.

Zig Ziglar told a story of a doctor, who on many occasions, struggled with getting drunk and hitting his wife. The next morning, he would wake up and see what he had done to his wife and be filled with remorse and promise her it would never happen again. But it did. The last time it was different. When the man woke and sobered up, he saw his wife sitting there with a black eye. He started in with his usual speech about how sorry he was and it wouldn't happen again. The difference with this occasion was the wife didn't look upset this time. No tears or pleading for change. In fact, she seemed calm. She reassured her husband with kind words, something along the lines of, "I know dear, I know it will never happen again . . . because I had a friend take a picture of my face. If she ever sees another bruise on me, she will be mailing a copy of that picture to all your patients. So I, too, believe it will never happen again." Ziglar shared how the doctor managed to find a self-control that he had never been able to obtain before that moment.[1]

In Matthew 18:15–17, it says,

> If another believer sins against you, go privately and point out the offense. If the other person listens and confesses it, you have won that person back. But if you are unsuccessful, take one or two others with you and go back again, so that everything you say may be confirmed by two or three witnesses. If the person still refuses to listen, take your case to the church. Then if he or she won't accept the church's decision, treat that person as a pagan or a corrupt tax collector.

This passage makes it clear that we are not to look the other way, deny reality or the truth, or wring our hands and wonder why God doesn't do something. Rather, *it places the responsibility on us*. We are told to confront sin.

So when my husband finished yelling at me and finally paused, I calmly responded from the peace the Lord had given me. I told him, "Honey, I want to share something with you. First of all, I give you my word, regardless of how you speak to me, I will speak respectfully to you (not because my husband deserved it, but I was following the example in set in Scripture[2])." I continued to share with my husband, "The Lord has been convicting me that I am to fear no man, and that even means not living in fear of you. I can no longer cower and submit to your angry outbursts. I really do want you to succeed; that is why I am sharing this with you now, so you won't be caught off guard the next time this happens. The next time you ask me to do something and it is attached to a f— you, or an angry you-are-an-idiot tone of voice, I'm letting you know in advance that that is my cue: I will be doing the exact opposite.

There is one more thing I need you to know. I am really tired of you breaking my stuff and throwing my things out. The next time you do that, I am going to ask myself who would Scott be really embarrassed to know that this is how he treats his wife behind closed doors. That is who will be getting a call from me. And you need to know you will not be able to make me feel guilty as if I betrayed you because I am letting you know in advance. The decision is completely yours."

On the inside, I was pleading, *Please, don't make me do this*. Nothing in me wanted to have to follow through with that. I never wanted to hurt him, embarrass him, but I felt God strongly calling me to hold my husband accountable and stop saving him from life consequences.

I am *not* endorsing to embarrass your husband publicly. Rather, I chose one person whom I knew would protect me due to the regard my husband had for this person. This does not mean go and tell everyone to humiliate him.

We see God throughout the Bible bringing things out into the light, not to shame but in hopes of bringing repentance. Deliberate public humiliation would not honor God, nor would God honor that action. However, I do see in Scripture the use of positive peer pressure to help turn someone back to godly behavior.

The next day, Scott came into the kitchen and grabbed my upper arm, squeezing tightly to get my attention. He had never done that before. He told me, "I am sorry for yelling at you, but don't you *ever* ask me if I am watching porn again."

I pulled my arm away and told him, "I will ask you whenever I feel the Lord tells me to ask you," and walked away. I felt a little shaken because he was trying to intimidate me but returning to what I felt God had called me to do brought my peace back.

I had to trust in the Lord's providence while being willing to risk divorce by using boundaries. Gary Thomas, author of *When to Walk Away*, clearly expressed in a blog post where your boundaries should be:

Consider this: if you have to compromise your morals, your faith in God, and your self-respect to "keep the peace," does the threat of being left alone really sound so bad? Remember, your God will

supply all your needs. If you follow his plan and still your
husband becomes one who rebels, God's provision and strength
will help you face the consequences. God won't leave you alone,
regardless of what happens. God, not your marital status, defines
your life.[3]

My walk in my marriage seemed similar to how Abraham was
listening to the Lord minute by minute when he was preparing to
sacrifice his son. It is important for us to do the same. Thankfully,
Abraham was not relying on an old word from the Lord but kept a
listening ear to the Lord. (see Genesis 22 for the complete story)

Earlier, in our 9/11 year, I felt the Lord tell me, "If you love me, you
will stay and show unconditional love." At that time, I wanted to leave
my husband so I could be emotionally OK and feel more comfortable,
but I felt like the Lord said no. I will be forever grateful He did, not just
because of the outcome I get to enjoy now, but I would have missed the
Lord showing me that his Word is true. He really is able to give peace
when there is no reason for it.

Now, a few months later, the Lord asked me to risk everything I
valued in my life. I had to be willing to leave if I wanted to save my
marriage, willing to risk it all to help deliver his son Scott, whom he had
crazy love for as well.

But I was scared. I remember telling the Lord, "I don't want to, Lord.
His yelling doesn't even bother me anymore. Now you want me to leave
just because he is watching porn?" I had to ask myself if porn really was
that big of a deal. Of course, now I know just how big of a deal it is, but
at the time I questioned it.

Looking back, I am so humbled by the goodness of God. He knew
my husband's problem was bigger than going to a few porn sites. I did
not. It is so important to follow the Lord's leading. He sees the whole
picture when we do not. I know we want a life recipe with very specific
directions that reads, "When they do this, you immediately do this, and
the guaranteed result will be this."

I really wrestled with the thought of having my kids grow up with
divorced parents. The thought of being a single mom was scary; the

thought of my kids being co-parented by another person (potential future girlfriend or stepmom) and having no say in the matter, even scarier! But just as God later wanted me to be willing to go to Iraq twenty miles from the ISIS capital when it made no sense to me, God was asking me to follow him into turbulent waters, no matter the cost. I am so grateful I did in both scenarios.

I would like to add a disclaimer/warning/encouragement. I am not recommending you threaten to leave your husband the first time you find your husband watching porn. I am saying seek God and his wisdom. I would find out years later Scott's problem was much bigger than I realized. God knew that history; I did not. There were those who thought I was extreme in my actions. All I could do was share that I was just trying to be obedient to what I felt like the Lord was telling me. That's all any of us can do.

A few years later after my discovery of Scott's online porn sites, my husband relapsed. I found many websites he had visited. I asked the Lord for wisdom on how to handle that situation and felt like the Lord said to show grace. So when Scott was coming off shift one morning, I had a nice homemade breakfast waiting for him with a printout of what I had found next to his plate. I left for a quick grocery run (so I could pray for strength and wisdom), came home, and told him how much I loved him and his desire to be a man of integrity. We talked about how to get back on track. We had recently purchased a new computer, and he had asked me to install the accountability software that only I would have the password to. Unfortunately, I had put it on the "I'll get to it eventually" list. I felt I had not been a good helpmate.[4]

There would be a couple of other relapses over the years leading up to Scott's complete deliverance. But I was able to handle these painful regressive periods because he had a genuine intention and desire to change.

I don't think there has ever been a time in history when it has been more difficult to be a godly wife. The ability to fulfill a desire is almost instantaneous. I am grateful I can't make brownies pop out of my phone instantly. The effort to make or buy them sometimes gives me just enough time to realize I don't want the results of that decision. With today's technology, our fellow brothers and sisters aren't always afforded that delay. Grace, coupled with strong boundaries, I believe is our best hope at attaining freedom.

13

FREEDOM DAY

"For the Lord is the Spirit, and wherever the Spirit of the Lord is, there is freedom."

2 CORINTHIANS 3:17

IT'S CHRISTMAS MORNING: 6:08 a.m. to be exact. I've been postponing starting this chapter because I just couldn't figure out how to begin. As I'm lying in bed, the house completely quiet with two out of three kids home for the holiday, I can clearly remember how one Christmas looked so different from where we are today.

I had no idea there was a deliverance in our family's near future. It was a beautiful, messy moment in our lives I will never forget. But just like in childbirth, there was a lot of pain but with no epidural in sight before the delivery would be complete.

The hard labor pains for this impending delivery started in early December. Scott kept Fred away for the most part for several years. Since I had established those boundaries about breaking and throwing my things away, he had done well.

Earlier that year, Scott went on a mission trip with our church to Hungary. We had been leading some small groups on marriage at our church. Life was good. In the months leading up to Christmas, though, I saw him reverting back to his old ways. Scott started getting mad easily. He would be fine one minute and then lose it over something simple the next minute.

Our children noticed the change and leaned on me when they needed help. When our oldest tried to open the office blinds, they got stuck. He called me in and asked for help because he was scared of his dad finding out. I tried to fix them, but instead of going down, I just got them stuck up farther. Scott came in and tried to lower them and when they wouldn't, started yelling at us.

"Why would you do this? Why didn't you leave them alone!"

I told him I was sorry, that I expected blinds to operate as they were supposed to. I didn't do anything crazy like trying to swing from them. We just tried to open them to let sunlight in. (OK, I didn't really say the swinging part out loud, but I thought it.) He was way too mad for any clever comments, so I was quiet as he ripped them out of the wall and threw them across the room.

We were planning to go to a church luau (aka a Hawaiian party) that night. It was taking place at a beautiful house overlooking the city. I was so looking forward to spending time with other parents but not with Fred. When Scott lost his temper, I told the kids to get in the car. "Time to go to Grandma's house!" I asked the Lord for wisdom on what to do and felt like the healthy decision I could make in this situation was to continue with the plan of an evening being with my church family, of swimming and BBQ. Knowing Scott wouldn't go with me, I wasn't going to leave the kids home alone with him.

As I drove the kids to Grandma's house, the kids talked about being scared of their dad when he got like this. They hadn't seen this side of him for quite a while, and it had caught them off guard. I prayed for wisdom as I drove and explained to the kids, trying to encourage them the best I could while not bad-mouthing their father. "We love Daddy, but Daddy does have some struggles with his temper, and it is OK for us to remove ourselves from the situation."

We needed to let Scott regain some emotional self-control. Because when he would get like this, he would berate me or the kids. It wouldn't be healthy for him to treat the kids that way or for them to see Scott lecture me and have them think that is how to treat women. That would be a bad example for my boys and for my daughter to think that was acceptable. I shared how we are all weak in different areas of our life and need to seek the Lord to help us improve in those areas. "So we will pray the Lord will help Daddy break free of his temper."

Scott began to realize the effect his temper had on our kids. Our oldest kept an electric scooter he rode to school parked in the garage right next to my husband's brand-new truck. (For some reason, I feel like I don't even need to tell you the rest of the story.) Yep, one day when my son went to move his scooter, he tripped, accidentally hit the accelerator, and dented my husband's truck. He came running to tell me, so scared to tell his father. I told him to go to his room. I needed to pray and ask for wisdom on how to best handle this. I called my friend Gina and told her to pray. This couldn't have happened at a worse time. Scott was already in Fred mode. I went in my room and prayed a quick prayer for wisdom and felt like God gave me the word to share with my husband. It went something like this.

"Scott, I need to share something with you. Our son just accidently tripped while trying to move his scooter and fell with his hand on the accelerator and hit your truck. He is currently waiting in his room, scared. You can do one of two things: you can go in his room and be that little boy's hero and show him he is more important than a truck, or you can crush him with your words. I pray you choose the first," and walked out. Thank God, he actually handled it with love for his son and didn't get mad at him. I've heard Scott retell that story of how much it affected him to see his son scared of him.

But the grand finale before the death of Fred started on December 2nd while putting up the Christmas tree. Our middle guy tried to take a picture of Scott and me in front of the tree, using his new phone we had just got him. Unfortunately, it slipped out of his small hands. That was all it took for Fred to manifest instantly.

I had a flashback to when our oldest was in the third grade, and we were going to surprise him with his first phone (the kind with only four buttons pre-programmed to call parents and grandparents). Scott called him inside from playing, but right when he was about to hand the brown paper bag to him, he didn't like the expression on our son's face, so he threw the bag at him and called him a little sh—. I stood there not knowing what to do. We are told to submit and never say anything negative about our husbands and only praise them, but seriously? What should have been a fun surprise turned into this?

So I stepped in right away, not wanting a repeat with our second boy. I got between him and our middle guy and told him, "Scott, you are not going to do this. You are not going to berate him for an accident. He was not being careless. Go take a moment to cool down if you need to." That was all it took for him to not speak to me for the rest of the month.

Hurtful words have a way of staying with a person for many years. Sometimes people can underestimate the power of emotional abuse and how destructive it can be. I found this interesting quote from the book *The Insanity of God*, comparing physical abuse to emotional abuse. Ripkin stated, "Their stories reminded me of something that I had seen in Somaliland and had confirmed again in some of the interviews that I had already done in Russia and other former Iron Curtain countries in Eastern Europe: The psychological aspect of persecution often causes deeper wounds and leaves greater scars than physical mistreatment."[1]

Well, after stepping in, regardless of being as respectful as I could, it didn't matter. Scott would not make eye contact with me or speak to me for the rest of the month. I continued to pray for my husband during this time. I was leading a women's Bible study, and one morning after study, my pastor and an elder dropped by the room. I broke down and started crying and shared with them our history and that I just didn't know what to do.

During one of my prayer times, I felt like the Lord told me I was not to continue and try to talk to Scott but to leave him alone with the Lord. I felt the Lord gave me a Scripture from Philemon 1:15–16: "It seems you lost Onesimus for a little while so that you could have him back forever. He is no longer like a slave to you. He is more than a slave, for he is a beloved brother, especially to me. Now he will mean much more to you, both as a man and as a brother in the Lord." I asked my pastor, "Am I doing the right thing? Am I alright with God?"

Nothing was more important to me than knowing my actions were honoring God. As much as I hated it when my husband was upset at me, the thought of something interfering with my relationship with God was more than I could bear. I shared how I had put up boundaries in the past, but that I was still the one who always initiated trying to get us back together.

I will be forever grateful that we were under a godly pastor who understood how to handle abusive situations. Scott would tell you how pivotal he was in our testimony and how things could've turned out so differently had he given me different advice. I have to share that part with you. For some, his advice will be considered controversial.

He reassured me that I was doing the right thing and I was OK in God's eyes. I wasn't being a disobedient wife. In fact, he took it further and told me, "Anna, men are hunters by nature. You play hardball with Scott. Don't go to him. Anna, I even mean sex. Don't be having sex with him while he is behaving this way."

Wow! That blew me away. I can't tell you how many times I would try and get my husband to love me again by doing sexual things and some that were not God honoring, all in hopes of regaining his love. Sometimes it would work, other times, afterward, he would just roll over and continue to ignore me. I felt so horrible. Marriage is a mutual submission. I am cautious with sharing this because I am aware how there are women who aren't honoring God, using sex as a weapon against their husband. As a power grab. This is not what we are talking about here. *Please, please,* understand the difference. I'm not talking about, "You made me mad, therefore no sex for you, buddy!"

I was conveying a message that was reinforcing Scott's abusive behavior. "Treat my wife horrible, mean, and ignore her, and she will do whatever I want in the bedroom." That is not a godly message to be sending. Thankfully, my pastor stopped that destructive thinking that day.

So that is what I did. I put my husband in the Lord's hands. At night I would go and read big God stories and pray. But honestly, I was wearing down. We were at the fifteen-year mark of marriage. Year after year, my husband would stop speaking to me for sometimes a month or longer if I made him mad over something like, "Please don't yell horrible things at our children for accidentally dropping a phone." I was so done I almost wished I would find out Scott had been unfaithful to me, so I could leave him and know for sure I was OK with God. I was tired of being treated this way.

During that round, he broke my favorite nativity set that I had kept from childhood. Scott said it was an accident, but my son came in the house saying, "Dad is mad and throwing things." Yet in the midst of this, I had a surreal calmness, almost like the Lord was preparing me for something big.

For the first time in my marriage, I was too tired to pray for him anymore. I've probably already mentioned how grateful I am for all my friends who prayed for us over the years. I will never forget being at a dear friend's house. Her husband was a police officer, so our husbands had a special EMS friendship. I shared with my girlfriend for the first time in my life I didn't have another prayer left in me. At that she dropped to her knees by her couch and took up our cause to Jesus for me. I'm tearing up now even thinking about that moment. They were getting ready to move hours away. The night before they moved, I remember her husband tearing up over our situation, hurting for the both of us. He loved his brother Scott. He offered to go talk to him, but I shared that I had tried that in the past, and I was holding on to the Scripture the Lord had given me in Philemon.

The weekend before Christmas was the yearly fireman Christmas party. Saying I looked forward to it seems too weak of a statement. It was a formal dinner up in the mountains at a well-known college's alumni resort. Each room had a fireplace, sitting room, bedroom downstairs, and an upstairs loft bedroom and bathroom. Snow on the ground and Christmas lights everywhere. The dinner was always amazing. It was formal attire. Every year I looked forward to shopping for my dress.

As the day approached, I sensed that Scott was planning on not going, because he knew how important it was to me. He had a history of not only breaking items that I valued but breaking plans that were important to me as well when he would get like this.

I know this next part is going to be controversial to some and seem extremely unwise. However, I sought God through this time and felt like I was supposed to go. So, I planned ahead and asked a girlfriend if she would go with me when he backed out.

The morning we were to leave, Scott saw me prepare my dress. He said nothing about not going until I asked, "What time do you want to start heading up to the mountains?" He looked up at me and just said, "I'm not going," and looked back down at what he was doing. I remained calm and told him, "Oh, OK, will you do me a favor though? Make sure to leave me the truck when you go and run errands. I hear there is going to be a lot of snow in the mountains, so I think I'll drive that instead of the car."

With that I started packing my stuff in the truck. The kids were already staying with their grandparents, so I concentrated on getting ready. I packed my worship music to play in the room, my Bible and journal, and my formal dress. My friend went with me. At dinner people would ask where Scott was. I made sure not to speak anything negative about Scott. I would tell them, "He wasn't feeling well and wasn't up to coming tonight, but how grateful I am that my friend could keep me company. I look forward to this night all year long. It is so lovely up here. What a treat to get to stay in beautiful accommodations." Then I would change the subject to what a beautiful evening it was.

At dinner I sat with some of our fellow Christian firefighter couples. Afterward there was dancing until early in the morning, but I excused myself and went back to my room while my friend stayed and visited longer. It left me hours alone with the Lord up in the mountains. I listened to worship music, read my Bible, and prayed for my family. It was a wonderful night of intercession. I remember thinking I wouldn't be able to sleep with my anxiety. I was surprised I had the courage to follow through with this and go to the mountains without Scott. I never went anywhere without him. I had always suffered from travel anxiety my whole life. This was really big on many levels for me to go alone. But I had peace in my room that night. I was even able to fall asleep, which was incredible. It turned into a sweet getaway with the Lord.

I went home the next morning to unfortunately more of the same. Scott didn't acknowledge me or speak one word to me when I came home. But I came home with a grateful heart for the time I was able to get away with the Lord. There is a Scripture painted on a board that hangs on the wall in our family room. I was thinking how to put into words my experience with the Lord on that mountaintop, and I think this Scripture describes it perfectly: "I have found the one whom my soul loves." (paraphrase of Song of Solomon 3:4)

The final week leading up to Christmas was uneventful. More of the same. That was until Christmas Eve. I was driving home from the store, talking with the Lord, when all of a sudden, I heard that still small voice very clearly say, "Scott has his own Facebook page." I thought no way. This was a big deal because up until this point, we had always agreed to share a page. We had seen how social media had broken up some of our friends' marriages, because what was once an innocent conversation with old friends turned into so much more.

We both agreed that if we were going to be a part of this new social media thing, this was the best way for us to handle it. In fact, a girlfriend's husband told her how he tried talking with me on Facebook, but I wasn't very talkative. After knowing me in person how chatty I could be, he thought maybe I didn't like him. His wife was in my Bible study, so she knew my views on being close friends with the opposite sex and explained to him, "Honey, it's not you. Anna won't chitchat with the opposite sex in private settings." It blessed me she knew that and also that she was able to explain to her husband it was not personal. Scott and I agreed on this philosophy . . . in principle anyways. So for him to have a Facebook page was a *huge* breach of trust.

As soon as I parked the car, I went straight to the computer and searched my husband's name on Facebook. His picture immediately popped up. My heart began racing wildly as I noticed he only had one friend so far, and it was a woman who was very pretty and single. Her description was, "I like to work hard and play hard." I walked out of the office and straight to the neighbors' house. We had been friends with them for years. He was one of my husband's first roommates.

Unfortunately for my neighbor, his wife was not home. Poor guy. Before I even asked if his wife was home (I know I just broke previously stated rule, but . . . I got nothing for you. I just did), when he opened the door, I just walked in and fell to the ground, crying, saying, "It is over." I told him about finding Scott starting a Facebook page and his only friend was a single woman. I asked if the kids could come over for a while so I could talk with Scott.

After the kids left the house, I approached him. He saw my face and tears and asked what was wrong. "Go into the office right now and open up your Facebook page." I saw he had created it only the previous day. I clicked on the private messages. He had messaged her with some small talk about his life and ended it with how good she looked. He tried to dismiss it as innocent.

"Don't even talk to me. There is only one reason you would start this without telling me when we agreed to share a page. You were fishing for a hookup. It was not your integrity that has prevented it but God! Is this an old girlfriend?"

He responded, "Yes."

"Is this a past girlfriend you have had sex with? And so help me, don't you lie to me! I have told you before I cannot tolerate lies."

"Yes."

I left and went for a drive. I called my pastor and told him we were finished. I had put up with a lot. I had tried to be the best godly wife I could be, but I wouldn't stick around for an unfaithful husband.

It was bad enough a couple of years ago I found out he went to a website where its whole purpose was for adults to hook up with one another. I told Scott that day if he ever went there again, I would divorce him. I would not stick around for him to bring another STD home to me. My pastor, of course, tried to calm and encourage me.

When I went home, I found Scott sitting in the office. I told him to be sure not to take any overtime on his six days off he had coming up. I told him I might be flying out to Texas. My best friend lived there. I needed time to think. I had some life decisions I needed to make. Then I walked out. If this thing were going to end in divorce, I felt like it was better to start it in my mid-thirties instead of finally figuring it out in my fifties that my husband couldn't remain faithful. Even though it would be hard, I could go back to school and live with my parents for a while.

The next day was Christmas. I had a strange peace, which was so unlike me. I told Scott when we got up that morning that today needed to be about the kids. We would not be discussing any life issues today. My daughter told me she wanted to spend Christmas day at a retirement home, visiting old people who might not have any family around. She literally drew fifty unique pictures to hand out there. So Scott, our daughter, and I went to visit and hand out pictures.

While we were sitting and having lunch with the residents, one older lady swore Scott had taken her out to lunch the week before, even though they had never met before. Through our conversation, we could tell she suffered from memory problems. But Scott just looked at me and said, "I swear that is not true." It made me laugh.

We made it through the day. By God's mercy and grace, I was able to enjoy being with my kids and have dinner at my family's house. I don't remember too much from the next two days, but I do remember Scott walking in while I was getting ready. I was crying, but I was going to suck it up because after the 9/11 year, I swore to myself I would never let him see me cry over him again. Yet I felt like I wasn't supposed to hide it from him but let him see that he hurt me. All I could say with tears running down my face was, "You broke my heart."

The following day after running some errands, I went to find Scott to ask him something. I had called for him, but he wasn't answering. I checked all over the house but couldn't find him. I don't know what made me look in his closet, but there he was lying face-down. The top half of his body covered by the hanging clothes. I said, "Scott, are you alright?" No answer. "Scott, are you alright?" I started to worry. That was the closet we kept our guns in. I immediately left and once again gathered the kids quickly and said, "Do not ask me any questions right now, but I need you to go to the neighbors' house right now. I will come for you in a little while."

All I could think of was how two of my dad's best friends shot themselves, and how the year before one of my friends came home to find her husband had done the same. If that was what I was about to find,

I did not want my kids in the house to see it. Once they were out of the house, I went back into the closet, but by then I could hear Scott crying. He still wouldn't answer me when I called his name.

Finally, he answered when I asked him, "Scott, did you hurt yourself?" He said no, he was fine. Once I knew he was fine, I shut the door and walked away and called our pastor. I told him that Scott might be ready to talk with him now. "You will find him in the closet."

He said he would be right over. Meanwhile, I called Gina and told her what happened. She said, "Don't you think you should go sit with him?"

"No, God can comfort him."

That was crazy out of character for me. In the past, if Scott would show the slightest sign of remorse for anything, I would instantly forgive and want to just forget about it and move on. In fact, in most instances throughout our marriage before then, I don't remember him ever saying sorry for something unless it was followed by an explanation about how it was really my fault that ultimately caused him to do whatever it was he did. In the past, if he just made me laugh or showed me an ounce of affection, that was all I needed—no apology necessary.

Not this time.

Our pastor and his wife showed up. I met them outside and told them that Scott was now sitting in the office. "Also, be prepared to be lied to." Up until this point, my husband would admit to partial truths in front of others but never own up to anything unless backed into a corner, so to speak. I waited, sitting on the curb with my pastor's wife. I told her, "You know, after today, my husband won't want to be your friend anymore because you know too much about us. Just so you know, I will still love you guys. I'm not going to give up any more friends because my husband is embarrassed by his actions. The Lord has grown me past that."

Pastor came out and asked me to come inside. He told me that Scott had admitted to everything I had shared with him. I was surprised. When I walked in, Scott just sat quietly in the chair. He looked pretty stone-faced, which produced the same response in me. I can't remember too much that was said, other than Scott saying I had already made up my mind to leave. Pastor explained that is not what I had said I wanted.

I explained how I saw what happened to Scott's mom and how I saw Scott following his dad's pattern. How Scott's dad would purposefully find objects important to his mother and break them or just randomly take her favorite things and throw them away to mess with her. (I found it interesting to learn later how Scott was never aware of his father doing this to his mother.) His temper and infidelities. Once I mentioned his father, he broke. Collapsed on the floor in sobs. I didn't know what to do. I know the one other time I saw Scott cry when I mentioned his dad beating his mom was during the 9/11 year. I had tried to hug him then, but he pushed me away and didn't want me near him. So I sat there watching him sob. It took Pastor encouraging me to go over to him that I went down on the floor and put my hand on his back. Once I touched him, I, too, broke into sobs with him.

He cried like never before. Scott describes this as a Romans 8:26 moment. "And the Holy Spirit helps us in our weakness. For example, we don't know what God wants us to pray for. But the Holy Spirit prays for us with groanings that cannot be expressed in words."

It was a from-the-gut cry. Scott would later share with me that in that moment he had a recurring vision that he had first had on a mission trip to Hungary. In the vision, he saw his dad beating his mom. It was very vivid to the point where he was even hearing the sounds he used to hear during those times, only this time he saw Jesus there on scene. Jesus looked at Scott (Scott always mentions how Jesus called him by name) and said, "Scott, I know this is hard for you, but I never left your mom and dad, and I always loved them."

Scott would later describe to me why the vision meant so much to him. "I liked it because God didn't make any excuses, called me by name, empathetically acknowledged it was difficult. Two other truths: he reaffirmed he never left my mom and dad and always loved them."

That was the moment that God healed a life wound with a supernatural release.

I'm not sure how much time had passed when we rose off the ground. Right after that, Pastor stuck out his hand and said to him, "Will you still be my friend?" That meant the world to Scott. He couldn't understand why he would want to be friends with a "dirty sinner."

My husband hit the ground that day and came up a new man. Never to be the same.

Right after Pastor left, we decided on the spur of the moment to go to Las Vegas to see "Phantom of the Opera." We had always talked about wanting to see that show together and had looked at going for our anniversary, but it just never happened. So we got in the car and made the drive. As we were sitting in traffic, I started to panic because at this time, I didn't know for sure if a life change had happened. I thought, *What have I just done?*

As I was starting to question the wisdom of this impromptu trip, I felt like the Lord spoke Scripture to me: "He looked at them and said, 'Go show yourselves to the priests.' And as they went, they were cleansed of their leprosy." (Luke 17:14) The lepers received their healing while on the road, but on faith they started down the road before they saw the healing. (I can feel the counselors cringe. I cringe with you; it does not follow protocol. But I really didn't know what I was doing. I didn't have or know any counselors other than the Holy Spirit.)

I felt the Spirit calm me down and speak to me, "It is okay, Anna. This time it will be different because you are different. If the change is not for real, I will guide you in your new life."

Thankfully, the change was for real. That weekend, other than watching "Phantom of the Opera" and eating at the restaurant directly next to our elevator for every meal, we never left our room. We spent our time crying and praying together.

We came home and did a forty-day media fast. I would fall asleep at night to Scott reading big God stories to me.

We both wanted a fresh start. The bedroom set we had was one Scott had before he ever met me. With Hebrews 13:4 in mind, "Marriage should be honored by all, and the marriage bed kept pure" (NIV), we went shopping for a new bedroom set. It was special to me for so many reasons, one being I had never had the opportunity to pick out a bedroom set. I am the youngest in my family, and although I was very grateful, I always had the hand-me-downs. Scott made the mistake of saying I could pick out any one I wanted. So I did!

It looked like a bed made for royalty. *Huge* four posts, with beautiful carvings on each one and a canopy top. I really wish you could have seen it! For years, many times I would walk into our bedroom and be in awe of what a beautiful set it was. The nightstands and dresser all had matching carvings. Fit for a queen. I always picked a purple comforter set because purple represents royalty. I was a daughter of the King of kings and would not compromise again for the love of mere man. It was my symbol of help of what God had done in our life.

We moved to a smaller, much older home to be closer to a refugee community. I felt like the Lord was telling me we were to lighten our earthly load—that he had called us to be transient people. That was a hard move because, in case you haven't figured it out yet, I am an emotional hoarder. Not of expensive things. Just things that I have attached a memory to. Although it was hard for me to release the set, it was very easy for the rest of the family who had to move those beasty posts every time we moved!

Also, after the Vegas trip, my husband put together a box with a picture of me on it from our trip and put little slips of paper in it. At random times he would write love notes, thank-you notes, or Scriptures to me. Following his lead, I bought him a treasure box and did the same for him. That tradition has continued for many years now. A newfound love for each other was brought to fruition after Freedom Day, and even though we still have our occasional arguments, Fred is dead.

14

REVELATION DAY

"And you will know the truth, and the truth will set you free."

JOHN 8:32

AFTER FREEDOM DAY, Scott has never been the same. When he got up off the ground, he was different in a beautiful way. God had changed him and it stuck. He no longer seemed to white-knuckle his temper. I saw his attitude change toward purity from "how close to the line can I get and still be OK with God and my wife" to "how holy and honoring can I be to this Jesus I love so much." He turned into such a consistently gentle, loving husband. He became the godliest man I know.

When we moved to our new home, the pastor at our church knew part of our testimony and told us about a conference that was in town called Pure Desire.[1] He thought Scott might be interested in a ministry that helps men break free from sexual addictions. Before we had ever heard of this ministry, I was pretty wowed by the transformation in Scott's life. I figured I was living as good as it could possibly get.

Scott went the first day to the Pure Desire conference by himself. We didn't know that wives could and should also attend. He invited me to join him for the second day. It was so eye opening to discover the depth of the problem in our churches, much less society as a whole.

Although I found the conference very interesting, I really didn't want anything to do with the ministry because it just seemed too overwhelming. Not only that, but I felt that although Scott and I had been through a lot, he had never physically cheated on me before. I wanted nothing to do with helping women whose husbands had sexual addictions. After all, Scott had done a lot, but he had never physically cheated on me, so what could I possibly offer these women?

I had seen firsthand the devastation that unfaithfulness can cause in friends' and families' marriages. That is a level of pain much deeper than I would ever know what to do with.

Yet I had also had a front-row seat to what unforgiveness looks like, and it is ugly. It will take your sound mind. I knew if I ever found myself in such a position, biblically and for my own well-being, I would somehow have to forgive. But forgiving and sticking around after such a betrayal of unfaithfulness are two different things.

Seeing how the fire department could be a "girls gone wild" environment for a lot of firemen, it crossed my mind frequently that I would potentially have to deal with that. My pre-plan solution was I would just leave. But fortunately, we made it safely through those years that Scott worked at the fire department with only one close call. Or so I thought.

One Tuesday night, Scott and I were lying in bed, ready to go to sleep, and I was thinking about a meeting we had scheduled the next morning regarding how to best help persecuted Christians. I was thinking to myself how different we were from those who were in prison for their faith. As I was remembering all that the Lord had brought us through, I remember saying to myself something I felt like I had said hundreds of times: "At least Scott has never cheated on me." It was almost instantaneously I heard the Lord speak to my spirit, "That is not true." What? I told myself to go to sleep—that's just crazy talk. I put it out of my mind and did just that.

The next morning, I woke up and went into the bathroom. I remembered the last time the Lord told me something when I was in the shower that I thought was crazy and became true. "Oh man! Last night when the Lord told me, 'That's not true,' it was shower clear!" That inner voice sounded the same as that day in the shower. *OK, Lord, I hear you, I hear you.* But the unfaithfulness had to have happened years ago.

Scott had been a transformed man for close to five years. There was no reason for me to think of that. There were no obvious signs. "Lord, I *know* I heard you. I believe you. But I've always said that is the one thing I would never forgive. That is a guaranteed 'I am leaving and never looking back.'" Would I really leave him now? I thought to myself, *I have had a pretty consistent, amazing husband for five years. So patient and kind, passionate for the Lord. No, I can't imagine walking from the man he is today.*

So I told the Lord, "Thanks for the update. I heard you loud and clear, but as the saying goes, we're just going to let dead dogs lie. What's in the past can stay in the past—no need to bring it up." I walked out to the office to open the blinds and let some sunshine in. I looked down and saw a Scripture card Scott had written on the desk. It read, "Do not lie to each other, since you have taken off your old self with its practices." (Colossians 3:9, NIV) It was as if the Lord was speaking to me.

"Lord, you're killing me here! Fine, you don't want us to lie to one another; I won't lie to you either. I'm too scared to know. I saw what it did to someone dear to me. Eighteen years ago, when she found out about her husband's unfaithfulness, it was as if who she was died inside of her. I saw what it did to another one of my dear friends, one of the strongest women I know. She wasted away looking like she came out of a prison camp for a while because the pain was too great for her to handle. So Lord, I have seen this kind of information crush stronger women than I. Since you seem to be anti-lying, I'll tell you the truth! I'm too scared to know."

I can't explain it, but I just felt like the Lord told me to table it and go to our meeting that morning. So Scott and I went.

Right after Scott and I sat down at the table, Scott shared a Scripture that had ministered to him in his morning devotions. Then someone else at the table shared, "You know what Scripture really ministered to me this morning? It is Psalm 112:7: 'They will have no fear of bad news;

their hearts are steadfast, trusting in the Lord.'" It was as if the Lord spoke directly to my heart. All of a sudden, I wasn't scared of the news anymore. I knew the Lord God Almighty could walk me through this. Right after she shared the Scripture, I flashed back to a previous meeting when we were discussing how an organization was threatening to "dig up dirt" on someone.

Right in that moment, it made perfect sense why this needed to come out more than it just being the right thing to do. It is the goodness of the Lord that brings the things that are hidden out into the light. I thought, *If we are in ministry, it needs to come out. People can't dig up what has been set out before them.* In that moment, I had complete peace and understanding with a whole lot of holy awe of how big God is.

"For all that is secret will eventually be brought into the open, and everything that is concealed will be brought to light and made known to all." (Luke 8:17)

I admit I don't remember much of what else was discussed at the meeting that day. All I could think about was talking to Scott afterward. As soon as the meeting was over, we got into the car. Before Scott had a chance to start the engine, I turned to him and told him that before we went anywhere, we needed to have a talk.

"Scott, the Lord has told me something. You need to know I argued with the Lord, telling him I didn't want to know the answer." I went through what I had been hearing from the Lord. "So Scott, this is not me asking, but God wants it out." The Lord enabled me to say with such peace and calmness, "Scott, the Lord wants me to tell you I will not leave you, and I will forgive you, but the Lord wants this out in the open. Have you been unfaithful to me in our marriage?"

He stuck out his hand as if to shake on it and said, "Do I have your word on it?"

Even though I absolutely knew it was true before I ever asked him the question, it still really hurt to hear it. I took his hand and started to cry and said, "Yes, you do. It's really going to suck. It's going to tear my heart out, but yes, you have my word, so get it out."

It was the 9/11 year of 2001. He had crossed paths with an old acquaintance. It had lasted two weeks, and he decided he couldn't continue to do that to me. He shared how he had become really angry that year. I was changing and falling in love with the Lord, turning into such a godly woman. He told himself if I wasn't going to be the fun he wanted, then he would find someone who would be. Of course, he profusely apologized and said he was an idiot and it was 100 percent his fault, I didn't deserve it, and so on.

I really don't remember much after that except that we went to the store on our way home. For the life of me, I can't remember what we needed that couldn't wait. I think maybe I just wanted to go to a place and feel normal for a minute before I faced my new reality. Maybe I just thought nothing heals a broken heart like one of their really good hotdogs. For whatever reason, my next memory is being in an aisle of a giant warehouse store by ourselves and just breaking down and crying. Him hugging me there and apologizing some more. We went home.

I went to my room and cried some more. *I don't even know where to begin. How could there be this hidden secret for so many years? Who was she? What did she look like?* So many questions rushed into my head and heart. *Oh, Lord, help me. I don't know what to do with this shattered heart that is inside of me.* But God knew this day would come and had provision waiting for me sitting on my dresser before I ever knew I would have a need for it. Oh, how the Lord spoils me.

I had recently ordered the women's curriculum of Pure Desire called *Betrayal and Beyond.* I received the books on a Monday. I remember telling the Lord when I was looking at buying them, "Lord, I just don't have the heart for this." Looking back now on that time, I can picture the Lord smiling and saying, "Don't worry, just like an Amazon order, your heart for this ministry is scheduled to arrive Wednesday morning."

On my dresser was not only the book but a leader's DVD. I put the DVD on and started to watch Diane, the wife of Ted Roberts, who wrote the curriculum of Pure Desire. I wanted to ask Scott so many questions. I heard Diane say that it would be easier for the wife to heal if she didn't ask unnecessary questions. She said the wife needed to know "who" only if she was going to come in contact with that person.[2] We had moved to another state.

Because of that advice, I decided I would not ask who she was. To this day I don't know. My best friend who had also walked this path agreed with that advice. When you know too many details, it paints a too detailed picture in your mind to overcome. Knowing does not make it easier but harder.

If you are dealing with this issue, I encourage you to seek the Lord's advice on how you should handle your situation. "If you need wisdom, ask our generous God, and he will give it to you. He will not rebuke you for asking." (James 1:5) You'll have that verse memorized by the end of this.

As I was watching the DVD, Diane went on to share how their church has a ministry to pastors who have fallen in this area. When pastors arrive, all of them are required to submit to a polygraph test. She shared that typically whatever the husband has shared with the wife is usually just the tip of the iceberg. There is usually more. The husband is usually too ashamed to come clean all at once. They call it a staggered disclosure. They teach the men in the Pure Desire group how that is the worst way to do it. The wives then live with wondering where is the bottom and if there more is on the way.[3]

Right when she talked about the iceberg analogy, I questioned, *Could there be more?* I felt a little fear rise inside me, but God reminded me of Psalm 112:7.

I smiled and said, "That's right, Lord. Sorry, I temporarily forgot. I do not fear bad news." I walked out of my room and told Scott to research someone who would be able to administer a polygraph test. I told him if it was good enough for the leadership at Pure Desire, it was good enough for us. He seemed to have no problem with the idea, so I felt confident in the moment that I knew everything.

Prior to Revelation Day, Scott and I had both been fasting and praying. During this time, Scott had been feeling the Lord convict him of the story of Achan.

In the book of Joshua chapter 7, Joshua asked the Lord about why they had lost a battle. Joshua was distraught at the loss of his men's lives. The Lord revealed to Joshua the reason for their defeat and loss of innocent lives was because of hidden sin in the camp. Someone had stolen some items and buried them in their tent. The man who had done that was named Achan. Joshua told Achan, "My son, give glory to the Lord, the God of Israel, by telling the truth." (v. 19) Because of Achan's sin, many innocent lives were lost.

Scott felt the Lord say it was time to remove *all* hidden sin. He prayed, "If this is you, Lord, asking me to tell her, then give me a sign. Have her ask me if I have ever been unfaithful to her. I saw what it did to someone we love dearly, and I don't want that to happen to her. I don't want to hurt her, so if you really want me to tell her, have her ask me."

There was no reason for me to ask, but God wanted me to.

About six months after our Revelation Day conversation, I called a dear friend of mine, Sarah. She is a few years younger than I and a tiny little thing who is a powerhouse in the Lord. I updated her on what the Lord had revealed to me. I kept waiting to hear surprise in her voice. Instead she said, "I am so sorry. I have to tell you something. About six months ago, the Lord woke me up in the middle of the night. I had a dream that Scott had been unfaithful to you and God wanted me to call and tell you. I just couldn't do it. I had no proof. You just don't call someone and tell them that. I was disobedient. I am so sorry. Instead, I just stayed up praying for you and your marriage. I have been interceding for you these last few months."

I was floored. I told her not to worry because I felt her prayers. Honestly, I'm grateful God told me himself. It was a little less awkward than having my friend tell me. It added to my wonder and awe of God. That is the main reason for wanting to share my story. As my niece said the night she met Jesus, "God is real!" It has been during my biggest trials and hurts when I have experienced God the most. It makes me confident I have a heavenly Father who loves and cares for me.

Scott and I went to our Friday appointment with a young couple trying to save their marriage. I shared with the wife what the Lord had revealed to me that week. I was no longer in some sort of teacher role, but we were now, as she put it that day, "battle buddies." I love that term. No one should be alone in battle.

On the drive home, Scott and I talked about our meeting with the couple. We had a polygraph scheduled for the following week. Something in my spirit was telling me there was something he was leaving out. I started to feel nervous at just the thought of there being more. That's when I told him that if there was something more he wasn't telling me, and I had to wait for a polygraph to find out, it would not end well for us.

He responded, "Can we talk when we get home?"

I will not give an accurate account of my exact wording. Just know some pre-Jesus words came out of me. I told him to pull over somewhere because I didn't want to have this talk with any kids in the house.

We pulled into a parking lot. He shared with me that there was one more thing not as bad as the first (his words not mine). We had only been married about three years at the time. I was also pregnant with our second son. There were no signs of any unhappiness that I could remember for the most part. He was very loving and kind during this time of our marriage. Relationally, I thought we were doing really well. Career-wise, this was during the time they were threatening layoffs of all the firemen because of lack of funding for the city. Scott was under a lot of stress.

It had happened right around the time we first got the internet in our house. We are talking dial-up here. (You could go clean a bathroom in the time it took to connect.) Unfortunately, Scott had started talking with a woman in a chat room. One night after he was done teaching a fire college class at a local college, he drove about forty-five minutes to meet up with her.

This one act probably hurt the worst out of everything in our marriage. After his confession, I inserted a couple more pre-Jesus words and told him to take me home. When I got home, I changed my clothes and went to the gym. I think ever since the 9/11 year, when I became overwhelmed with anxiety, I learned how we treat our bodies affects our mind. I knew if I was going to have a high-stress situation, I would need to make sure not to turn to my sugar addiction and exercise to get some nerves out at the gym.

I walked into the gym and saw some men working out. I thought, *Lord, I know how some women who have been in my place decide they will seek revenge on their husbands by having an affair on them. Lord, I'm not saying I'm above that because you and I both know that as soon as I think I am above something, I am all in. I'm just saying right now, in this moment, I see these men working out trying to make their muscles even bigger just so they can get with more women. They are all a bunch of liars!* I went on the treadmill for a little bit and went back home.

When I arrived home, I went to my room, grabbed my Bible, tossed it on my bed, and sobbed. I cried out to the Lord with my broken heart. In that moment, there were three things I brought to the Lord: (1) "Lord, I have forgiven my husband of *so* much over the years and now you are telling me there is more! I don't have any more forgiveness in me." (2) I repeated my gym sentiment to the Lord and felt angry as I said, "All men are liars!" (3) I felt so sad looking over our marriage at how I had kept such wide boundaries between me and other men. I told the Lord, "I have wasted my faithfulness on a man who never cherished it. Not only did he not cherish it, he made fun of me and got angry at me for being too extreme in how I kept my distance from the opposite sex." I did this not because I was saintly but because I always knew what I was capable of.

The thought of hurting my relationship with God and my husband brought fear and sadness. I cherished both so dearly I wanted to protect both. It would always hurt me when my husband didn't seem to value that quality in me. Scott is the only man I had ever been with. I had always saved myself for my future husband, and it was an irreplaceable gift that I felt was wasted that day. My very soul ached. Through blurry, tear-filled eyes, I randomly opened my Bible.

It fell open to Psalm 116. The top of the page started with verse 5: "The Lord is gracious and righteous; our God is full of compassion. The Lord protects the simplehearted; when I was in great need, he saved me." (NIV)

That made me smile because I always refer to myself as a simple woman, and in that moment, I, too, was in great need.

"Be at rest once more, O my soul, for the Lord has been good to you." (v. 7, NIV)

This verse was as if God himself were speaking to me: "I know this is hard for you, my sweet daughter, but I am with you. You have one more in you. This additional disclosure will not break you. I am with you."

There is something about being in God's presence. You can make it through more than you could ever imagine with the presence of God. I was in a state of complete brokenness, but God showed up on the scene, and my scene began to change with the words to rest because of the goodness of the Lord. *Yes, Lord, you have always been good to me.*

"For you, O Lord, have delivered my soul from death, my eyes from tears, my feet from stumbling, that I may walk before the Lord in the land of the living. I believed therefore I said, I am greatly afflicted. And in my dismay I said, 'All men are liars.'" (vv. 8–11, NIV)

In one of my most broken moments, I couldn't help but look up and laugh and say out loud, "You get me, Lord." Once again, I felt the goodness of the Lord's presence increase in my situation, and gratefulness started to coexist with my brokenness. I read on.

"How can I repay the Lord for all his goodness to me?" (v. 12, NIV)

I paused and started recalling all of the goodness the Lord had shown me throughout my lifetime—not just this day but every day.

"I will lift up the cup of salvation and call on the name of the Lord. I will fulfill my vows to the Lord in the presence of all his people." (vv. 13–14, NIV)

Right there! The Lord answered my three points of brokenness I brought to him. I hurt so deeply that I felt I had wasted almost twenty years of faithfulness on someone who didn't value it. I would never regain those years. You can't regift your life. I started recalling all of God's faithful moments, and there were too many to count. How do you repay a God who has been so faithful to you when you haven't been 100 percent faithful to him? Like me?

The words brought me back to the vows I had made to God in the presence of a whole lot of people. On my wedding day, I didn't just make vows to remain faithful to Scott but also to God. Once again in that moment, the Lord spoke to my heart, saying to me, "Anna, you did not waste your faithfulness all those years, because your faithfulness was never to Scott; it was to me, and being faithful to me is *never* a waste!" That day I wrote that in my Bible next to those verses, so I would never forget.

Healing didn't come overnight, but it did come.

15

POLYGRAPHS

WE SAT down to talk to a radio show host about our story. Everything was going well until we mentioned how polygraphs can play a crucial role in the recovery from sexual addiction. His attitude suddenly changed from being very interested to "Don't call us—we'll call you."

Christians are sometimes surprised by the use of this tool. Some Christians believe polygraphs mean you are not trusting Jesus. I disagree.

During a Pure Desire conference, I felt the Lord prompt me to offer to pay for a young couple to have a polygraph. While sitting on the opposite side of the room from this couple, I prayed, *I don't even know if they want a polygraph. Lord, would you give me confirmation that this is you?* After saying that to the Lord, the young wife raised her hand to ask Dr. Ted Roberts, "When is it a good time to have your spouse polygraphed?" I quietly giggled to myself, thinking once again, *Lord, you spoil me with ridiculous provision.*

At break time I told her what I felt the Lord had shared and that we would love to pay for their polygraph. She was so grateful. The husband was grateful after it was over. They worked with a counselor to help walk them through the process and face the results. That was a few years ago. They are still together and view the polygraph as a helpful tool in their healing.

Polygraphs are not necessary for every situation; perhaps if there isn't a history of porn addiction or infidelity. I compare the decision to how we approach the detection of cancer. My mom had breast cancer at age thirty. Due to our family history, it was recommended I have mammograms starting in my early twenties. I have never had a Christian tell me I am not trusting Jesus by having one. It is common knowledge that the earlier you catch cancer, the higher the chance of recovery. So every year I get a mammogram. Not because I have a fear of cancer; it's just a wise tool to employ due to my family history.

We see an example in the Bible of what trusting God looks like while upholding accountability. The Israelites had been living in captivity in Babylon for seventy years. They were being allowed to return home loaded with gold, silver, and supplies.

Ezra called everyone to fast and humble themselves before God and pray for a safe journey to Jerusalem. Ezra said,

> For I was ashamed to ask the king for soldiers and horsemen to accompany us and protect us from enemies along the way. After all, we had told the king, "Our God's hand of protection is on all who worship him, but his fierce anger rages against those who abandon him." So we fasted and earnestly prayed that our God would take care of us, and he heard our prayer. (Ezra 8:22–23)

What great faith Ezra had in trusting God for their safety. Right after that declaration of faith and answered prayer, Ezra shared how he appointed twelve leaders of the priests to be in charge of transporting all their valuables. Right before handing everything over to their care, Ezra said, "I weighed the treasure as I gave it to them and found the totals to be as follows." (v. 26a) Then he went on to list each of those weights. But his message to the priests didn't end there. Before they set out on their journey, he informed them what would happen when they arrived (boundaries) and reminded them of who they were.

> And I said to these priests, "You and these treasures have been set apart as holy to the Lord. This silver and gold is a voluntary

offering to the Lord, the God of our ancestors. Guard these treasures well until you present them to the leading priests, the Levites, and the leaders of Israel, *who will weigh them* at the storerooms of the Lord's Temple in Jerusalem." (Ezra 8:28–29, emphasis mine)

Ezra reminded the Israelites of being set apart for the Lord (just as husband and wife have vowed to be set apart for each other and for the Lord). Ezra knew the human heart's vulnerability to be tempted to steal what was not their own, and he helped the people resist by letting them know of the boundary he had placed in advance. If anything had gone missing, Ezra would have found out because he was going to use a scale (polygraph) to confirm they had succeeded in remaining holy before the Lord.

As the Russian proverb that was made well known by President Reagan during nuclear deals with Russia says, "Trust but verify." That is what we see Ezra doing here. Ezra took representing God and his name incredibly seriously. He refused to ask for soldiers to protect them but instead chose to fast and pray for protection. When it came to his own priests, he trusted God but still used a scale to verify their honesty.

Ezra recorded that the people and goods were protected during their journey. That was a miracle. Everyone in the area probably heard about the Israelites getting to return to Jerusalem with many valuables. After such a victory of the Lord's protection, one might think Ezra would feel the boundary of accountability he placed on the priests to be unnecessary. But on the fourth day after their arrival, all the valuables were weighed at the Temple, just as Ezra said they would. He trusted but verified. "Everything was accounted for by number and weight, and the total weight was officially recorded." (v. 34a)

The priests kept themselves set apart and holy for the Lord's service, without a record of one priest saying to Ezra, "Why don't you trust us?" Honest people don't mind accountability.

That's why random drug testing doesn't bother me in the slightest because I don't use drugs. People with nothing to hide, hide nothing. "For all that is secret will eventually be brought into the open, and everything that is concealed will be brought to light and made known to all." (Luke 8:17)

The stakes are very high in your marriage, and it is wise for you to use all tools at your disposal. Sexual addiction causes terrible destruction to a family and its future generations. If getting a polygraph is something you think would be helpful for your marriage, I highly suggest making sure you do it with the help of a counselor who works with addictions. Should there be things revealed that you did not know about, it is wise to have someone ready to help you wade through those rough waters.

It has been over ten years since Scott's Freedom Day. We don't have a set schedule to be polygraphed. It is just known that I can ask for one at any time. Scott has passed all with flying colors. Scott told me the man who administered his test asked him on his last one, "Do you ever lie to your wife?" Scott answered, "No, it's not worth it!"

I'm not planning on asking for any more polygraphs, but if I were, it wouldn't be an issue. Scott doesn't care. He has been transformed.

16

REJECTION OR PROTECTION?

"Come, my people, enter your chambers, and shut your doors behind you; hide yourselves for a little while until the fury has passed by."

ISAIAH 26:20 (ESV)

WHEN YOU FIND out your husband has been unfaithful, you're immediately thrown into a situation where ministries can be destroyed and friends reject you. Your heart is so injured during that time that sometimes the rejection of others is perceived and other times it is real. Regardless of which category yours might fall in, you can hold on to the sweetness and protection spoken of in this Scripture: "You hide them in the shelter of your presence, safe from those who conspire against them. You shelter them in your presence, far from accusing tongues." (Psalm 31:20)

I'm going to take a wild guess that you, too, have had times where you were rejected by people you love or highly respect. But what if God is really protecting us from something? Let me share with you how a rejection turned out to be the best redirection that I will forever be grateful for. Without this experience, I would've missed out on a life-changing trip to Iraq. But in the moment, all I could see was rejection.

Ever since my 9/11 year, I have been passionate about the persecuted church. I have felt indebted to them, because without their examples of honoring God in difficult circumstances, our family might not still be intact. Every opportunity I would get I would share stories of Christians, who like the disciples in the Bible, proclaimed Jesus even if it cost them their lives. I have always wanted to help them however I could, so whenever I was asked to speak somewhere, whatever payment I received I donated to an organization that helped bring relief or supplies to Christians in persecuted nations. I owe the persecuted church so much that nothing would bring me such joy as having an opportunity to raise awareness and funds to help them. I shared about my passion with every pastor or pastor's wife I met. Even strangers on airplanes. I was able to get a particular ministry several bookings at churches. Once Scott retired and we relocated, I planned to apply as an official representative of this organization.

Right before we started the process, a friend called to ask if I had heard about one of their main leaders committing suicide because the police were coming to arrest him for charges of molesting a young girl. I was shocked. Not this man! This man had spent time in a foreign prison for Jesus when his plane crashed. I read his book about the experience. He was a powerhouse for the Lord. How could he fall so far?

I became filled with such sadness and a holy fear that no one is immune to falling. I remember thinking, *Do I want to still try and represent an organization whose leader could do such a thing?* I did, because regardless of what he had done, the persecuted still needed help. Scott and I submitted our applications and started the interview process. Yet early on, something felt off. I remember telling my friends, "You know, I can't explain it, but I think they are going to turn us down. There is nothing in the natural I can think of that would make them turn us down. You can call any church we have ever been at or any organization we have worked with. We come with good references."

The Lord had granted us favor with everyone from the organization we had met in person. However, I had never met the one doing the phone interviews, and we didn't really mesh well. She ran on the serious side, and if you haven't figured out already . . . me, not so much. I knew we would be a different fit from their usual applicants, but I knew this passion to serve my persecuted family was God's design and call for me. Even if I am Dori's twin from *Finding Nemo*!

Here is the supernatural part. We submitted our audio presentation through email for her to review. When she opened it, she couldn't hear anything on the file. We sent it to other people for both Mac and PC. Everyone else could open it and hear it. So, the interviewer asked for a thumb drive. We mailed a thumb drive. She heard nothing when she plugged it in. So we sent her a CD. You probably guessed it already. Even though we checked it and could hear it just fine, she heard nothing when she played it.

The interviewer was starting to get frustrated with me. It seemed as though she thought I was somehow being dishonest with them. We were friends with one of their representatives who stayed at our house a few years back. I wanted to call him because he knew us in person, not just from a phone conversation. He had written us a beautiful thank-you card telling us, "I normally don't have time to write thank-you cards, but the Lukes are not normal people." I wanted to photocopy it and send it to the person interviewing us. Yet I felt the Lord kept telling me, "Don't defend yourself; just trust me."

Well, the end result was the interviewer sent me an email declining our application. Right before I received the email, my middle son, who is a man of *very* few words (I have no idea how we managed to breed a quiet one with the rest of us chatties), hugged me one night when I started crying. I had just hung up the phone with the interviewer and said, "I think they are going to turn us down." My sweet son hugged me and hesitantly said, "Mom, I don't think God wants you to do this." I knew he was right when he spoke that but just couldn't understand why.

When they sent my rejection email, I was so sad and heartbroken. Throughout the process, even though I felt like the interviewer and I probably weren't clicking, I just kept telling myself, "Wait until she hears my presentation." I am the first to confess how incredibly nervous I get when speaking, so I'm sure I didn't inspire confidence in someone who had never met me. Knowing that God helps me when I speak, I figured things would smooth out when she heard my presentation. She never had that opportunity because I believe the Lord supernaturally worked it out that way. I just didn't understand why at the time.

After sharing what happened with one of our pastor friends, he told me, "Why don't you just go anyway? You don't need their permission to go speak about the persecuted church and the organizations that you like." He wasn't talking about collecting money—just advertising to get people involved. Somehow that felt like breaking "the Rules." I don't know what Rules exactly, but I didn't want to break even imaginary ones.

The following day I continued feeling very sad and rejected. I was getting ready to go have my quiet time with the Lord, so I asked him, "What am I supposed to do now? What can I do with no official organization to represent?" As I walked into my closet, my eyes lowered, and I saw a book I had read a few years ago tucked back under the hanging clothes—*The God Smuggler* by Brother Andrew. It was his life story of how he started smuggling Bibles into communist countries. It was filled with miraculous stories of God's protection. There was also an interesting detail about his story that I didn't remember until I felt the Lord nudge me to pick up the book and open it. Brother Andrew was turned down by two different missionary organizations. I had forgotten that detail until I randomly opened to a page with a sentence highlighted on it. It read, "What can one man do with no money and no organization to represent?"[1]

The very words I had just used to ask God the same question. The answer was Brother Andrew went anyway. He went out in faith and with no official organization to represent. That was God's answer to me: "Go anyway. Serve the hurting and the persecuted wherever I open a door for you."

This led me to contacting someone else who was working with persecuted Christians. I shared how I spoke at churches and wanted to know their opinion on which organizations were doing a good job at helping the persecuted church.

On the way to the meeting, I thought, *What if they say to me, "You know what organization you should work with is _______ (the one that just turned me down)."* I was feeling embarrassed. After all, who gets turned down to work for free? It felt equivalent to calling a child sponsorship organization to sponsor a child and them replying, "I know these kids are desperate for help and are going to die if they don't get it, but they aren't that desperate to have someone like you. No thanks."

If people knew this organization had rejected me, would they automatically reject me too? The Lord reminded me of what he has always told me. That I am to live a transparent life, never try to be something I'm not to impress people, and let him decide who wants to work with me or not. With that in mind, I prayed, *If you want me to tell them about being turned down, just make it known to me when we meet, and I will. Otherwise, I'm not going to bring it up.*

As soon as we sat down and exchanged greetings, the first question was, "So, do you work for _______ organization?" Their question made me laugh because of God's continual faithfulness to answer my questions. So I kicked off the meeting with the very thing I thought I would be too embarrassed to tell them. But I loved God more than trying to save face.

"No, I do not. They didn't want me. I tried to, but they rejected me." To my surprise, they actually looked relieved.

They told me, "That was not God's rejection but God's protection."

That one phrase has had such an impact on our life. I can't think of one perceived or real rejection that has not worked out for my good and benefit. Our family has added to that quote to include God's redirection. Time and time again God has used man's rejection to redirect us to the exact position he wants us. I am so grateful for the Lord's faithful directions. He is more accurate than Google Maps!

Because I was turned down from the first organization, I was able to connect with a ministry that was a better fit and didn't require a personality transplant. I seriously thank God that he didn't say yes to the first group.

God continued to cover us with his protection. Before I knew my world was going to be rocked with the news of Scott's infidelities, I committed to a ministry trip that was scheduled for two months later. However, the trip was canceled after Scott's infidelities were revealed. It felt like extra rejection for my husband's life choices. I remember crying/complaining to the Lord, *Why do I have to pay for his sins? Why should I be sidelined because of his choices? I'm not the one who committed adultery.*

I later learned the cancellation had nothing to do with Scott's disclosure. Once again, it was not rejection but God's protection. If I had been traveling with that ministry, I think I would have just tried to brush the infidelity news under the proverbial carpet. It was God's love for me that prevented the opportunity from coming to pass. I needed to be home. My heart was more damaged than I cared to admit or could even realize at that time. I needed to heal.

Even David, in 1 Samuel, experienced rejection that was evidence of God's protection. A Philistine ruler, Achish, had to ask David and his men to stay out of a battle. David was surprised and demanded a reason. But Achish wouldn't budge.

> So Achish finally summoned David and said to him, "I swear by the Lord that you have been a trustworthy ally. I think you should go with me into battle, for I've never found a single flaw in you from the day you arrived until today. But the other Philistine rulers won't hear of it. Please don't upset them, but go back quietly." (1 Samuel 29:6–7)

David had done nothing wrong but had served faithfully. Even Achish testified as much. David didn't realize it at the time, but God was actually working for David's benefit by using man's rejection to move David where he was needed more.

David's response was similar to what we feel when we are rejected: "What have I done to deserve this treatment?" (v. 8) He didn't do anything to deserve it. God just knew more than he did. David and his men needed to be at home. Their families were in trouble.

Three days later, when David and his men arrived home at their town of Ziklag, they found that the Amalekites had made a raid into the Negev and Ziklag; they had crushed Ziklag and burned it to the ground. They had carried off the women and children and everyone else but without killing anyone.

When David and his men saw the ruins and realized what had happened to their families, they wept until they could weep no more. David's two wives, Ahinoam from Jezreel and Abigail, the widow of Nabal from Carmel, were among those captured. David was now in great danger because all his men were very bitter about losing their sons and daughters, and they began to talk of stoning him. But David found strength in the Lord his God. (1 Samuel 30:1–6)

Poor David could not seem to catch a break! I love the last line. It seemed everyone was against David, but it didn't break him because people were not his source of his strength. His God was.

Sometimes when it seems people are rejecting us, it may be God repositioning us to strengthen us for a rescue mission. Rescue missions are rarely easy. I needed to sit out from traveling to get strengthened for the battle God had called me to.

I now look back at these events that felt like personal rejection, and I am grateful beyond belief. My broken heart, just like a broken bone, needed to be casted and hidden away for a brief time so it had time to heal. I needed to Isaiah 26:20 it for a while: "Come, my people, enter your chambers, and shut your doors behind you; hide yourselves for a little while until the fury has passed by." (ESV)

17

GOD'S HEALING

"O Lord, if you heal me, I will be truly healed; if you save me, I will be truly saved. My praises are for you alone!"

JEREMIAH 17:14

I'VE SEEN firsthand how a broken heart left untreated can lead to a broken mind.

The Lord brought Revelation Day on April 17th, two days after the Boston bombing took place during the epic marathon. I remember sitting in front of the television as they showed pictures of those who had been injured. Some had even lost their legs in the explosion. The agony must have been unreal. Those people would never be the same. They would have to learn to live differently. How would they adapt? Would they be able to get past the emotional damage as well? Would they hold on to the emotional pain caused by the physical trauma?

After Scott's second disclosure, I felt like a bomb had gone off unexpectedly in my life, and I lost my emotional legs. I thought I would never view our marriage the same way. Pictures that I had once cherished —like when the kids were toddlers visiting him at the fire station, Scott holding them as they climbed on the fire engine—now seemed to have emotional slime on them I couldn't seem to rub off. For years these pictures brought me such joy, but now my first thought was he had already been with two other women by this time. Our happy memories now felt contaminated, infected with an incurable virus.

I returned to watching the news of the bombing victims. The Lord told me, "Anna, just like the victims you are watching, your healing won't be immediate. It will be painful. It will take work. You will need time in rehab, but I am designing a new set of legs for you as well. Believe me when I tell you, you will be able to do more with your new set of legs than you would ever be able to imagine."

The Lord often communicates with me through word pictures. I pictured the Olympic runner who had both legs amputated below the knee when he was only eleven months old. (I almost didn't include this analogy because he was convicted of murdering his girlfriend. But then I am reminded that the Bible is full of flawed people's life stories who did something really great one moment and something really horrible the next.)

Oscar Pistorius holds a few world records in the Paralympic Games and was the first double amputee to win an able-bodied world track medal in the 2011 World Championships. And the first double amputee to compete in the regular 2012 Olympics. Many fought against him competing in the regular Olympics because they said, due to his artificial limbs, he had an unfair advantage. Can you picture someone telling his mom while her baby was in the hospital getting his legs amputated that one day he would compete in track in the Olympics? Not only that, people are going to oppose it because his new legs will be considered an unfair advantage!

Beautiful things can come out of terrible experiences. The very thing that I thought would totally crush my heart and life was being used to help many others deal with their crisis. Scott has also used his healing and deliverance to lead many men to deal with their sexual addictions in Pure Desire groups.[1] It is so exciting to see my husband reach out to others and by God's amazing grace help them find their way to freedom.

But before I could operate in my "unfair advantage," I had to spend some time in emotional rehab. For some reason, because of how my husband's infidelities were revealed in such a miraculous way, I thought my healing would come instantaneously. It did not.

I didn't know how I could be fine and happy one moment and then out of nowhere something would trigger a flashback, followed by a racing heart and a flood of tears. I once heard it referred to PISD (post-infidelity stress disorder). Anger was another frequent visitor to Anna's emotional town. Unwelcome, uninvited, but a very present visitor.

A few days after my husband told me everything, I remember crying and telling him, "It is not fair that you get to be OK. I am a mess! You broke my heart, and I have no idea how to fix it. I have never seen anyone go through this in a healthy way. What would that even look like?"

Scott suggested I call our chiropractor's wife, who was very passionate for Jesus and an older (than me) woman. "She is such a loving wise woman. Why don't you call her and see if she can be of some comfort or has any advice?"

My husband, by this time, had held me and prayed with and for me numerous times. I just needed another woman to talk to. We had only lived in our new area less than two years at this time. I didn't have any long history friends nearby at the time. For my husband to not even care about his reputation or how he would look to our Christian chiropractor and his family spoke loudly to me about how much he had changed over the years. In the early years, he would cuss me out saying, "Don't you tell anyone our problems!" The man I am married to today showed no concern for protecting his reputation, as his priority was to help his wife find healing.

The Lord continued to provide for me before I ever knew provision was needed. I picked up the Pure Desire workbook called *Betrayal and Beyond*.[2] I had watched the leader's video and was getting ready to start working through the workbook. As I started to read through it, I decided I would like to go through it with other women. The group I found only had a couple of months left, but they kindly let me join. It was helpful having a place to speak freely.

After that was over, I decided to go to counseling. I wanted to see if the experts could shed any healing light on my situation. Here is a journal entry from the morning of my first appointment:

I had my first counseling appointment this morning. Pretty much was NOT looking forward to it. First time paying someone to listen to me. Once my friends get wind of this, I suspect I will probably start receiving bills from them for all the years they have had to listen to me. I'm hoping once they see how much tissue I use from my overproducing eyes and nose, they don't raise my rate. Kleenex isn't cheap.

On the way there, I was getting frustrated because I couldn't get the radio to change. I really wanted to listen to worship music on the way, but I was driving our son's car, and no matter what button I pushed, I couldn't get it to change. I then tried to turn it off by pressing the big circle knob—everyone knows that is how you turn a radio off. No go. As a song blares in my ears, "I'm already gone," I'm yelling back to it, "I'm not gone. It is just one counseling appointment!" No matter what I do, I cannot silence or change stations or just plain turn it off. I'm stuck!

I then thought—what a perfect word picture for where I was going this morning. I find myself a bit stuck, still with a hurting heart and memories and pictures that used to be so sweet to me. Now I find they have a slimy film on them, and I don't know how to change that. I have pressed every button, turned every knob I know how to, but I need someone to teach me how to change stations. So off to counseling I went.

I met my counselor. A sweet lady as I knew she would be. Of course, she knows firsthand of what it is like. I shared my story with her. She said this is one of the deepest wounds a woman can have. I agree. I told her I only know to describe it as a soul wound. She said for her she doesn't know if she will be completely healed until heaven, but it could be different for me.

I believe it is like my friend had it explained to her. It's like losing a child. You manage to go on and even maybe have more children, but you never forget about the one you lost. It won't always hurt this bad, but there will always be a little ache left behind.

I discussed with my counselor how long it was healthy to bring up my hurt to my husband. I viewed this in the context of seeing one of my dearest family members lose all emotional stability after she found out about her husband cheating on her. She spent the next twenty-plus years making him "pay." Always bringing it up, not only privately but at family gatherings. Even to strangers in grocery parking lots. Anybody who would listen.

I shared with the counselor I had had a front-row seat to that show. I had seen firsthand how unforgiveness took my relative's sound mind, and how that rage didn't stay contained only toward her spouse but affected every other relationship in her life. If I tried to encourage her and tell her that wasn't healthy, she got angry at me for "taking his side." Before she knew it, her woundedness pushed everyone she cared about away. I didn't want this to happen to me. Unforgiveness wasn't an option.

I love how my husband explains it to those he has mentored. There is a difference between forgiveness and healing. Being hurt doesn't mean you haven't forgiven. If someone gets stabbed in the chest with a knife, you can immediately forgive the person who stabbed you. But the healing process can take a very long time. That life-threatening (marriage-threatening) wound needs a long time to heal. It needs a lot of wound care and doctor visits. It doesn't just happen overnight.

I have seen the goodness of God more than this girl (me) deserves. I, in my naivety, thought I could move past this like a bad case of the flu. *It will be really hard for a while, then back on my feet I go.*

April 17

*Hello, my sweet Jesus. Oh, how I love your Word. It is such a
comfort to my soul. Most of the time I live in a space where I feel
completely healed, then out of nowhere something small can
bring up fear and anger. Scott told me yesterday how he spoke to
a woman who was a life coach at the coffee shop where he meets
weekly with some of his peer friends. She happened to be sitting
at the table next to them. It brought up anger in me. (I was
thinking that was just the type of woman my husband would like.)
It brought up so much fear and hurt and anger in me as I thought
about how Scott told me the woman he cheated on me with in '01
was just an acquaintance he ran into and in a two-week period
was sleeping with her. How does that happen? I just checked the
calendar and past journal entry. Today is the one-year
anniversary of my crushed heart.*

*Oh, how I had hoped it would have been completely healed by
now. Although we have made great improvement, my heart still
bleeds from being wounded so deeply. Today, I am crying pretty
hard.*

During this rough spell, the Lord led me to Lamentations 3:19–26:

I remember my affliction and my wandering, the bitterness and
the gall. I well remember them (*that is so me!*) and my soul is
downcast within me, yet this I call to mind and therefore I have
hope. (*The writer had to take an action of calling these next
statements to his mind, and because of that action he was not
without hope.*) Because of the Lord's great love we are not
consumed, for his compassions never fail. They are new every
morning; great is your faithfulness. I say to myself (*self-talk
matters*), "The Lord is my portion therefore I will wait for him."
The Lord is good to those whose hope is in him, to the one who
seeks him; it is good to wait quietly for the salvation of the Lord.
(NIV, additions mine)

This Scripture was almost like it was written on a doctor's prescription pad, so I wrote these words also in the margin. "Anna, your pain will not outlast God. Your broken heart has an expiration date on it. God wins in the end, not pain and tears." God had reminded me to not fear, my complete healing was coming, and to wait patiently on the Lord.

I love how Max Lucado wrote in his book *Before Amen*: "He will heal you, my friend. I pray he heals you instantly. He may choose to heal you gradually. But this much is sure: Jesus will heal us all ultimately. Wheelchairs, ointments, treatments and bandages are confiscated at the gateway to heaven. God's children will once again be whole."[3]

The Lord heals people differently, using different tools and different time frames. I met a lady who led a Bible study for a group of women, and her experience was radically different than mine. Her heart was instantly healed. No struggle whatsoever. I went home and prayed, asking the Lord if I was missing something. *Am I not as holy or mature as she is?* The Lord reassured me that he was in control of the process and timing.

Years later I became very grateful the Lord didn't heal me instantly. I would've missed out on all the memories of my husband patiently hugging me, praying for me when I had a random, rough moment. I wanted to be better. I didn't rage or yell when I would have a moment. I would more often than not just get quiet. He would recognize it and ask me, "Are you having a moment? Would you like me to pray with you?"

I would wonder, *How is he doing that? How is he not responding with, "Why don't you just let it go already?"* Instead, he responded as 1 Corinthians 13:4–7 says, with patience and kindness, over and over again. I didn't know how to stop the moments.

Scott was truly repentant of all the damage he had caused in the early years, and I would not bring the memories up again to him but would take every thought captive and make it obedient to Christ. (2 Corinthians 10:5) When the devil would try and remind me of who Scott was, I would remind the devil of who Scott is today.[4]

Who Scott is today I refer to as an Ephesians 3:20 husband.

∼

The summer following Revelation Day, we were on vacation in San Diego on Coronado where we used to camp with our kids. As we were walking in front of the Hotel Del Coronado, all of a sudden, old friends started randomly showing up. They would give me an excuse of why they happened to be three hours from where they lived at the exact time we were. I believed everyone until the fifth couple showed up. Scott had arranged for us to renew our vows on the beach with our pastor and his wife. We were able to celebrate with many of our close friends who had loved us through all of those difficult years.

After we returned home, I listened to our original wedding song, and instead of bringing me the usual warm fuzzies it used to, it made me feel sad. I thought, *Lord, will you help me with this? Should I just listen to it over and over again to try and get it to represent what it once did?* The Lord responded to me with this Scripture: "And no one puts new wine into old wineskins. For the old skins would burst from the pressure, spilling the wine and ruining the skins. New wine is stored in new wineskins so that both are preserved." (Matthew 9:17) Instead of trying to recreate the old, I decided to pick out a new song to represent the new people we had become. It is important to take time to process and heal, but there will eventually come a time when one needs to stop trying to live a new life using the old filter because "it will burst from the pressure." New wine is stored in new wineskins (new life), so that both of us can be preserved.

Neither one of us is the same person we married. Praise God! I like to think I'm not as emotionally needy. (I'm so glad there are no comment sections in the middle of books so my friends can't contest that statement.) My husband is no longer the angry adulterer. We have both been made new for a new life together. All glory to my sweet Jesus!

Whether you are trying to stay together or your marriage has landed in divorce, God wants to bring healing to you. Seek it out. Do whatever it takes. Don't be like Naaman in 2 Kings who almost missed out on his healing because he didn't like the instructions the man of God gave him.

God had used Naaman mightily, but there was a tiny problem with Naaman's awesomeness. He had leprosy. But leprosy wasn't his biggest problem—pride was.

So Naaman went with his horses and chariots and waited at the door of Elisha's house. But Elisha sent a messenger out to him with this message: "Go and wash yourself seven times in the Jordan River. Then your skin will be restored, and you will be healed of your leprosy." But Naaman became angry and stalked away. "I thought he would certainly come out to meet me!" he said. "I expected him to wave his hand over the leprosy and call on the name of the Lord his God and heal me!" (2 Kings 5:9–11)

Sometimes we can all have a little Naaman in us.

When we have been used by God or have been in church leadership for a few years, without realizing it, pride can have a way of sneaking into our thinking: I don't need help, or I don't want to let people know I'm struggling. I've been a Christian too long to need help.

In the midst of my first year of healing, I attended a Bible study, not as a leader but as a fellow student. I had led Bible studies for almost ten years at this point. But while getting ready that morning, I heard the Lord tell me to attend with a humble heart. On the first day, a lady burst into tears, brokenhearted because she had cheated on her husband and lost her marriage a year earlier because of it. She couldn't seem to heal. Everyone in the room prayed with her and encouraged her.

The following week during the video session, the Lord wanted me to ask her if she would pray with me and for me at the altar. After the video I approached her and explained that I was also suffering from a broken heart and was struggling to find healing. The Lord encouraged me that we should go pray together since Jesus said he came to heal the brokenhearted, and I didn't remember there being any stipulations on what caused the brokenness to begin with. Jesus was willing to start a healing work in both of us. So after everyone left, the two of us knelt at the altar and prayed for each other. That was the first moment I felt my heart turn the corner on the path to healing.

Thankfully, our friend Naaman listened to his servants and not his pride. Even though what he was asked to do for his healing didn't make any sense to him, he did it anyway. Read for yourself how his story ends.

But his officers tried to reason with him and said, "Sir, if the prophet had told you to do something very difficult, wouldn't you have done it? So you should certainly obey him when he says simply, 'Go and wash and be cured!'" So Naaman went down to the Jordan River and dipped himself seven times, as the man of God had instructed him. And his skin became as healthy as the skin of a young child, and he was healed! (2 Kings 5:13–14)

I love that his flesh was returned in better condition than if he had never had leprosy! This old guy got skin so clean it was compared to that of a young boy. I could use that kind of makeover! Moral of the story: seek out your healing with a humble heart trusting God's Word. Not only will your heart get healed, you might just find yourself coming out looking younger. It's good to hope.

18

SUBMISSION

"ME TOO." Those two words have been blowing up the internet. People are in shock, hearing the now not-so-secret stories of sexual and other abuses of power in Hollywood against the women who work in the media industry. Stories of actresses having to endure all sorts of sexual abuse and intimidation who were too scared to tell anyone for fear of the repercussions, loss of careers, or, even worse, having their names smeared. Some of the most popular male news anchors have lost their jobs because secrets have been brought out.

These stories are horrifying, but the ones that take the abuse to a whole other level of depravity is when the abuse happens in a church and someone attaches God's name to it. I guess I'm not the only one upset about it because #metoo has started a similar hashtag of #churchtoo.

In a panel discussion about the decline of Western culture, Dennis Prager, who is Jewish, asked a question he loves to ask pastors, priests, rabbis, or anyone who thinks about religion. "What is the greatest sin you can commit in your religion?" He stated that in his religion, you can ask any traditional rabbi even in his sleep and you will get the same answer: "Doing evil in God's name."[1]

According to Dennis and the rabbis he consulted, the statement of "Do not take God's name in vain" in the Torah (first five books of the

Old Testament) has been mistranslated. In their opinion, the more accurate translation is "Do not carry the Lord's name in vain." In other words, do not commit an evil and say you are doing it for God. He continued to say, "Nobody makes a case for atheism like someone who does evil in God's name," and "Nobody makes a case for God as beautifully as the one who does beautiful things in God's name."[2]

"When an irreligious person commits evil, it doesn't bring God and religion into disrepute. But when a religious person commits evil in God's name, he destroys the greatest hope for goodness on earth—belief in a God who demands goodness, and who morally judges people."[3]

I have come across many women who are married to abusive or sexually addicted men. Their husbands (worse yet, their pastors) sometimes have Ephesians 5:22–24 as their main life Scripture: "For wives, this means submit to your husbands as to the Lord. For a husband is the head of his wife as Christ is the head of the church. He is the Savior of his body, the church. As the church submits to Christ, so you wives should submit to your husbands in everything."

Those who hang all their theology on the "wives submit to your husband" verses alone use this passage to justify any action, regardless of the situation. Yet people who quote this passage typically leave out verse 21. Before wives submit to husbands, it says, "And further, submit to one another out of reverence for Christ."

One commentary expands on this Scripture with, "Paul devotes twice as many words to telling husbands to love their wives as to telling wives to submit to their husbands. How should a man love his wife? He should be willing to sacrifice everything for her, make her well-being of primary importance, and care for her as he cares for his own body."[4]

In a lot of cases, when a woman goes to her church and says she is being abused, whether physically or emotionally, she is oftentimes told to go home and pray for her husband and is reminded of her duty to submit. She is encouraged that prayer and submission will bring change.

When women are told to submit to anything their husband wants them to do, even when it's perversion, it forces the word "submit" to carry God's name in vain by putting a stamp of approval on something that is evil, which is "a stench in the nostrils of God." (James 4:17, ESV) As if God would condone a woman being forced against her will to do something that God is against!

Many women walk away from their faith because Scripture is misused to justify keeping women trapped in abuse. They then go through life saying, "If this is the God of the Bible, then I want nothing to do with him." If I hadn't studied God's Word for myself, I could have been counted among those women.

A young married girl I know was told by a respected, older pastor that she was supposed to submit to her husband no matter what. She was not even allowed to leave if she felt unsafe unless her husband said she could. Of course, my husband and I disagreed with the pastor and offered support to the young woman. I felt so sad.

I did what I always do when feeling high emotion—I went and spent time with my Father. I asked the Lord, "I am very aware of the 'wives submit' Scripture, but do you intend for wives to submit regardless of what their husbands do?" In true fashion, whenever I asked the Lord a question, he answered me by bringing Scripture to mind. I thought of Acts 5, the story of Ananias and Sapphira. I saw this story through new eyes.

Ananias and Sapphira sold a plot of land, and Ananias told the apostles he was donating all the profits from the sale. In reality, he kept some back for himself. He lied because he wanted to appear more generous and holy without backing it up. The result was instant death. Then his wife came to face Peter's questions, not knowing what had happened.

> Peter asked her, "Was this the price you and your husband
> received for your land?" "Yes," she replied, "that was the price."
> And Peter said, "How could the two of you even think of
> conspiring to test the Spirit of the Lord like this? The young men
> who buried your husband are just outside the door, and they will
> carry you out, too." Instantly, she fell to the floor and died. When
> the young men came in and saw that she was dead, they carried
> her out and buried her beside her husband. Great fear gripped the

entire church and everyone else who heard what had happened. (Acts 5:8–11)

I find it very interesting that Sapphira was called in separately from her husband. If submitting was everything, then she should have gotten a godly high-five with a "Way to go, Sapphira—at least you submitted to your husband's wishes." She was held accountable separately for her part, with the penalty being death. The two of them wanted to appear godlier than they actually were, and Sapphira was willing to help with the coverup.

Teaching women that godly women should cover for their husbands does not line up with Scripture. There are times where love covers a multitude of sins, but I don't believe abusive behavior falls under that. To cover the abuse is unloving to the abuser. It will hinder their chances for life transformation.

Many have walked away from belief in God after experiencing abuse in the church because of how it was handled by the church. Some women are told that if they let this get out, they could hurt the cause of Christ. What is extra painful is when a victim's own family members tell them this. Unfortunately, this happens all too often.

I can't help but wonder if the prophet Nathan had such pressure put on him when he confronted King David when his adultery and murder went public. Notice Nathan didn't go to Bathsheba and tell her, "I heard what happened between you and King David. You realize David is famous around the whole world. If you let this get out, YOU are going to make God look bad."

Not only did Nathan go straight to the source and hold the guilty party accountable, but it wasn't covered up at all. In fact, in 2 Samuel 12:12, Nathan told David, "You did it secretly, but I will make this happen to you openly in the sight of all Israel." Nathan also shared with David that he was forgiven, but there were still severe permanent consequences for his sin, including the death of his child. Even though David proved himself to be a man after God's own heart, it didn't get him out of having to walk through heartbreaking consequences of his choices. Thousands of years later, we still know about them. I believe they were left to us as an example that God isn't for coverups, but he is for true accountability, repentance, and when possible, restoration.

The submission passage in Ephesians 5:22–24 is similar to Romans 13:1–2, which says, "Everyone must submit to the governing authorities. For all authority comes from God, and those in positions of authority have been placed there by God. So anyone who rebels against authority is rebelling against what God has instituted, and they will be punished." And yet we see many examples of God blessing or affirming non-submission in particular situations.

How about the story of Abigail in 1 Samuel 25? Abigail was married to Nabal, a very rich man. The Bible describes these two very differently. Abigail was sensible and beautiful, but Nabal was crude and mean in everything he did. You can even add arrogant to the list of attributes as you read how he interacted with people. In this story, however, he wasn't dealing with just anyone; he was being crude, mean, and arrogant to the future king, David.

David asked Nabal for some provisions for him and his men for protecting Nabal's herds. Nabal's response was basically, "David who? Get out of here!" (v. 10, my paraphrase) Nabal picked the wrong guy to mess with because "Get your swords!" (v. 13) was David's reply as he strapped on his own. David and four hundred of his best friends/fighters headed out to wipe out Nabal and all who were with him.

This is when sensible and beautiful Abigail comes on the scene.

Meanwhile, one of Nabal's servants went to Abigail and told her, "David sent messengers from the wilderness to greet our master, but he screamed insults at them. These men have been very good to us, and we never suffered any harm from them. Nothing was stolen from us the whole time they were with us. In fact, day and night they were like a wall of protection to us and the sheep. You need to know this and figure out what to do, for there is going to be trouble for our master and his whole family. He's so ill-

tempered that no one can even talk to him!" (1 Samuel
25:14–17)

I see Abigail as a brave, godly rock star who had a huge impact on
my life. She was just told her husband didn't want to give David
anything. Abigail gathered a bunch of supplies to bring to David and his
men, but she didn't let Nabal know what she was doing. From what we
know about Nabal, it was probably dangerous for her to disobey his
orders. But she did it anyway because she felt it was the right thing to do.
Abigail did not submit to her husband's bad counsel.

> When Abigail saw David, she quickly got off her donkey and
> bowed low before him. She fell at his feet and said, "I accept all
> blame in this matter, my lord. Please listen to what I have to say. I
> know Nabal is a wicked and ill-tempered man; please don't pay
> any attention to him. He is a fool, just as his name suggests. But I
> never even saw the young men you sent." (vv. 23–25)

Abigail did not excuse his behavior with a "you don't know him the
way I do—he didn't mean it—he just had a bad day." She called him out
for what he was, an ill-tempered man and then some.

Before the Lord transformed me, I felt like my husband's press
secretary trying to hide any bad behavior by spinning it differently.[5] Not
Abigail. She wasn't going to have any of that. During a time of not being
under a man's protection and provision, it could have meant her very
survival. Not only that but when she returned home and found her
husband had been busy throwing a wild party, she waited for him to
sober up and told her husband what she had done.

David, a man after God's own heart, praised God that Abigail did not
submit to her husband's wishes and did the very thing she knew her
husband had already said no to. Because of such "rebellion" on her part,
lives were saved.

Let's bring the discussion up to more recent times. Today there's a lot
in the news about Christian bakers breaking the law by refusing to bake
cakes for same-sex weddings. They strongly believe baking a cake for a

same-sex couple would be dishonoring to God. So, despite Romans 13 saying we must submit to authorities, they chose to do otherwise.

A judge solemnly swears to perform all the duties incumbent upon them as under the constitution and laws of the United states. There have been a few judges refusing to perform a same-sex wedding, county clerks refusing to be part of issuing marriage certificates to same-sex couples. Companies refusing to offer abortion benefits even though the law states they are supposed to. The supreme court recently upheld a law forcing pharmacists to offer abortion pills. Many Christian pharmacists feel it goes against God's Word. There have been many occasions throughout history where man's law contradicts God's law.

Nik Ripkin shared something very interesting concerning Romans 13. After visiting a communist country, he found that the church wasn't suffering from much persecution. It looked positive at first, but then he discovered why.

> From the beginning of communist rule, this nation's churches quickly and completely embraced the verses that Paul wrote in Romans 13 about honoring and obeying the authority of earthly rulers. In fact, the churches emphasized those verses so much that they ignored and failed to obey many other scriptures, including some of the central teachings of Christ.[6]

That philosophy killed that church, just like focusing only on "wives submit to your husbands" as your main tenet kills marriages.

Yet because we are Christians, we are to honor authorities. Christians should be the best citizens in the whole world. By respecting authorities, we honor God as he asks us to do. But to take this Scripture as a rule to never disobey authority might be obeying the letter of the law, but it is not obeying the spirit of the law. (see 2 Corinthians 3:5–7)

Should Corrie ten Boom have obeyed the Nazis' orders instead of hiding Jews, trying to save them from torture and death? Should the African-American community have continued to comply without peaceful rebellion to segregation? Of course not! We are to fight against injustice. "And what does the Lord require of you? To act justly and to love mercy and to walk humbly with your God." (Micah 6:8, NIV) So to make a blanket statement that women should submit to their husband's requests regardless of their husband's behavior, I do not believe it is of God at all.

We even see that Jesus couldn't stop butting heads with church leaders because they thought he was breaking God's law. He saw a woman who had been doubled over for eighteen years and couldn't stand up straight. He healed her on the spot.

> But the leader in charge of the synagogue was indignant that Jesus had healed her on the Sabbath day. "There are six days of the week for working," he said to the crowd. "Come on those days to be healed, not on the Sabbath." But the Lord replied, "You hypocrites! Each of you works on the Sabbath day! Don't you untie your ox or your donkey from its stall on the Sabbath and lead it out for water? This dear woman, a daughter of Abraham, has been held in bondage by Satan for eighteen years. Isn't it right that she be released, even on the Sabbath?" This shamed his enemies, but all the people rejoiced at the wonderful things he did. (Luke 13:10–17)

I can't help myself, but did you see how he called her "this dear woman" followed by the knowledge of how long she was "held in bondage"? She must have felt forgotten for all those years, but that wasn't the truth. Jesus was aware of her pain and suffering. He made it known to her, "I am not going to make you wait one more day for freedom, no matter how mad I make the religious leaders" (my interpretation of that verse). Oh, how my heart melts at Jesus's compassion and gentleness.

We are not told the motives of the religious leader, other than he was mad because he felt Jesus was breaking the religious law. The leader was accurate in referring to the Lord's instructions to Moses (see Exodus 31). The Israelites were not to do any work on the Sabbath. The consequence was a serious enough violation that they would get the death penalty. The leader was just quoting what the Lord had told Moses. And yet the Son of God, God in the flesh, showed mercy for the "dear woman."

My dear sister, just as this woman was unable to stand straight on her own until Jesus healed her, go to Jesus for your touch and healing. When you are touched by Jesus and see how valuable you are to him, you, too, will be able to stand straight once again. And just like that woman, you won't be able to help but praise God.

Yes, we are to submit to our husbands and each other. Our husbands are called to love us as Christ loved the church. When submission is done how God intended it, motivated by love and without trying to control another person, it is a beautiful thing. Please do not let someone misuse Scripture to abuse you, and read for yourself about how Jesus interacted with women. I believe you, too, will fall in love with my Jesus.

19

———————————

BATTLE PLAN

> "You can only grow in jail what you take to jail with you.
> You can only grow in persecution what you take into it."[1]

CHINESE BROTHERS RELEASED FROM PRISON

THIS BOOK IS NOT INTENDED to be a play-by-play of what you should do in your situation. My main message is to seek God for what you should do in your situation. So this battle plan is just to share what I did during my marital troubles but also what I did to get over my anxiety concerning my trip to Iraq. I actually started writing this out as I was preparing to leave for my first trip to Iraq when ISIS was still in control of Mosul.

As someone who has struggled with anxiety, the only way I know how to not fear something and return to a peaceful mind is to play out the what-ifs in my head. I see it in my mind's eye, but in the midst of whatever the situation, I see Jesus standing in the middle of it. I ask him, "What now, Lord?" Then I feel him guide me through. So if my trip ended badly (i.e., kidnapped by ISIS), what would I need to get through it to remain faithful to the Lord until the end?

It was the same strategy I used to get through all our marriage struggles. Hopefully, it will be helpful to you as you seek God for wisdom in your unique life situation. After all, he is the only one who fully understands every detail of your life. If you find it helpful, print off a list of what is helpful for your plan of overcoming your situation.

Pray for God to send you a battle buddy.

If you have to run the risk of being kidnapped by ISIS, you want your best girlfriend to go with you. It's biblical, really. Jesus kept a few friends close. Right before his biggest trial, the cross, and right after the Last Supper, he went to pray. Knowing the time was near, he wanted a few of his closest friends with him. "Then Jesus went with them to the olive grove called Gethsemane, and he said, 'Sit here while I go over there to pray.' He took Peter and Zebedee's two sons, James and John, and he became anguished and distressed. He told them, 'My soul is crushed with grief to the point of death. Stay here and keep watch with me.'" (Matthew 26:36–38)

We weren't meant to go through our trials alone. "Two people are better off than one, for they can help each other succeed. If one person falls, the other can reach out and help. But someone who falls alone is in real trouble." (Ecclesiastes 4:9–10)

I love how Max Lucado puts it: "Lean on God's people, cancel your escape to the Himalayas. Forget the deserted island. This is no time to be a hermit. Be a barnacle on the boat of God's church. "For where two or three are gathered together in My name, I am there in the midst of them." (Matt. 18:20)[2] Max sure does have a way with words. Yes, my friend, go get your barnacle on! Invite someone to walk alongside you.

Always remind yourself you are a child of God.

Made in his image. Fearfully and wonderfully made. The enemy's sole purpose is to break you down. Many times he will use other people, even those closest to us, to try and accomplish his goal. Never forget your value in Christ.

My husband and I have been giving driving lessons to our friends who are newly arrived refugee girls from Syria. They are so much fun. My contribution to the lessons is to sit in back with whoever is waiting for her lesson, sharing snacks and visiting. I was telling my friend "M" that I had been eating too enthusiastically lately and needed to exercise because I was getting fat. She whispered to me, "Anna, do not say that in front of your husband." I whispered back to her, "M, I think he already knows!" It made me giggle. The thought that by not mentioning something, I could hide the obvious.

After her driving lesson, we took a picture together. When looking at it, I noticed a few more wrinkles than before and mentioned, "Wow. I'm getting older." Once again, my sweet M came across the room and whispered, "Anna, do not say that in front of your husband." I returned the whisper saying, "M, I think he knows that too!" I found the interaction so fascinating. I joke about getting older, but I don't mind. I love getting to live the life I do. The wrinkles just let me know I am getting closer to being with Jesus! That's a marvelous thing. It also is a reminder that I don't want to waste time because I want to bring as many as I can to live eternally with Jesus.

"And I am convinced that nothing can ever separate us from God's love. Neither death nor life, neither angels nor demons, neither our fears for today nor our worries about tomorrow—not even the powers of hell can separate us from God's love." (Romans 8:38a)

Not even wrinkles or fat can separate us from God's love! We get to operate from a position of being loved and valued regardless of what any man or woman may think of us.

It would take a whole other book to describe how valuable you are to Christ. May I suggest before reading another how-to-fix-your-marriage book, invest time into learning who you are in Christ. When your security is anchored in him, the world is such a brighter place.

Memorize worship songs.

When my mind is tempted to fear, I want it to default to worship instead. I am reminded of the story of when Paul and Silas were thrown in jail (see Acts 16). Their prayers and songs of praise were heard by God, and he sent an earthquake that threw open the doors to their cells. I know it can be hard when you don't feel like it, but put on some worship music and make a joyful noise unto the Lord, sweet sister.

> But as for me, I will sing about your power. Each morning I will sing with joy about your unfailing love. For you have been my refuge, a place of safety when I am in distress. O my Strength, to you I sing praises, for you, O God, are my refuge, the God who shows me unfailing love. (Psalm 59:16–17)

There is a peace that is found in singing, or in my case, humming. As we were getting closer to leaving for our trip to Iraq, I noticed I would start singing to myself or humming without realizing it. This is something I journaled two weeks before our trip.

> *I'm at the airport. While in the restroom, I didn't realize I was humming "Jesus Paid It All." A fellow hand-washer said to me, "Boy, you are happy today!" I just smiled at her. I'm sure she didn't have the time to invest in listening to me explain that it's more than happy. It is more like a desperation that has been covered with peace.*

> *While walking in the airport, I told my husband, "The next time we board a plane two weeks from now, we will be headed to Iraq." When I kiss my kids good-bye on that morning, I'm sure it won't be so quick—the hug will be a little longer, a little tighter. God hasn't promised me I get to come back. He has only spoken clearly I have to go. And to trust. Trust that he will be there waiting for me when I get off the plane. He promises me his presence.*

The Lord's presence is worth singing about. I am so grateful the Iraq trip happened in the middle of writing this because I was starting to question myself: "God, were you really that peace-giving to me during those dark marriage days?" I was worried that it was almost like telling a fishing story—with each telling, the fish tends to get bigger. Or like when your parents walked home in the snow, the house tended to get farther away each time.

I can tell you with certainty that God can give you peace even when your life is not peaceful, or in my case, preparing to go visit ISIS territory. That, my friend, is no fishing story! Don't underestimate the power of singing worship songs in the midst of your trials. Songs of worship change your perspective and bring you closer to God.

Spend time daily in God's Word.

I like to think of it as lie repellent. Jesus himself used the Word to combat Satan when he was tempting him to not trust the will of God.

Chinese believers will memorize whole books of the Bible in preparation for the prison ministry they know will come eventually. They call prison the school of theology, or seminary. They don't even really trust you until your faith has been tested in prison.

For me, the One Year Bible format works best. It doesn't matter what format you choose just as long as you get into the Word. I love devotional books, but never let them replace your time with the Bible.

Stand strong on the truth that God will work out everything for good (see Romans 8:28). "For the word of God is alive and powerful. It is sharper than the sharpest two-edged sword, cutting between soul and spirit, between joint and marrow. It exposes our innermost thoughts and desires." (Hebrews 4:12)

"Tribulation has always marked the trail of the true reformer."[3] I need to know God is doing something in the midst of my situation. It will be used for a good purpose, either for me only or to strengthen me so I can be used to strengthen others. In Luke 22, Jesus let Peter know that Satan had asked for permission to sift him (Satan had to ask permission because he is *not* in control). But Jesus prayed for Peter and told him when it was over to go and strengthen the others.

It's possible my situation may lead me into the presence of the Lord Almighty, Jesus Christ, for all eternity. Not a bad deal—no more tears, no more suffering. I want the invisible to be more real to me than the visible, like it was for Moses.

> He thought it was better to suffer for the sake of Christ than to own the treasures of Egypt, for he was looking ahead to his great reward. It was by faith that Moses left the land of Egypt, not fearing the king's anger. He kept right on going because he kept his eyes on the one who is invisible. (Hebrews 11:26–27)

Bring big faith to your battle.

One of my favorite answered-prayer stories came from the first refugee who lived with us. He was a Christian pastor from Iran. I cannot share his name with you or too many details of his life because he still has family over there. But I can share that he was one of many kids in his family. He and one of his brothers came into a relationship with Jesus. When his family found out, he was kicked out of the house at age sixteen. The Lord told him to go back, even though they were still very mean to him. He decided to pray and fast for forty days.

He said it was around the twentieth day when his mom was home alone in the apartment and heard a knock at the door. His mom answered and saw Jesus standing there. Jesus said, "Why are you persecuting my son ______ (called him by name)?" I will never view Revelation 3:20 where Jesus says, "I stand at the door and knock" the same way. Apparently, Jesus was serious about that. Amazing! His parents accepted the Lord and now have gone to be with Jesus. Prayer and fasting matter even when we can't see it in the natural.

While waiting for God to answer my prayers, I will feed my faith by recalling not only my answered prayers but those of others. I will wait confidently on the Lord for his guidance and provision. I will refuse the lie that prayer is a waste of time and a last resort. It will be my first resort knowing how important it was for Jesus himself to take time to pray. How much more important it is for me.

I also make sure to read about other people's big God stories as well. To have big faith, you have to continually stoke it with big God stories. A couple of my favorites to read are *The Cross and the Switchblade* and *The Heavenly Man.*[4]

Begin a prayer journal.

This step can help you bring big faith to the battle. I have given examples of my journaling in this book, but I would also like to give you Hezekiah's prayer as an example. In 2 Kings 19, right after Hezekiah received a message from the enemy telling him, "Don't let your God, in whom you trust, deceive you with promises" (v. 10), God's Word tells Hezekiah's response. It says he went right to the "Lord's Temple and spread it out before the Lord." (v. 14) I love that expression. When things get hard, we need to just "spread it out before the Lord." But read exactly what spreading it out looks like:

> After Hezekiah received the letter from the messengers and read it, he went up to the Lord's Temple and spread it out before the Lord. And Hezekiah prayed this prayer before the Lord: "O Lord, God of Israel, you are enthroned between the mighty cherubim! You alone are God of all the kingdoms of the earth. You alone created the heavens and the earth. Bend down, O Lord, and listen! Open your eyes, O Lord, and see! Listen to Sennacherib's words of defiance against the living God.

> "It is true, Lord, that the kings of Assyria have destroyed all these nations. And they have thrown the gods of these nations into the fire and burned them. But of course the Assyrians could destroy them! They were not gods at all—only idols of wood and stone shaped by human hands. Now, O Lord our God, rescue us from his power; then all the kingdoms of the earth will know that you alone, O Lord, are God." (2 Kings 19:14–19)

He began with declaring who God is. After spending some time securing the bigness of God in his mind, he followed up with a "it is true, Lord." This situation may look bad from a human standpoint but not from where you stand, or should I say sit? That's pretty cool. God is so powerful that he doesn't even have to get out of his chair. He spoke the whole world into existence.

Your struggles have not gone unnoticed. Lock eyes with Jesus and spread it out before the Lord with big faith in the one who spoke the world into existence. Start your day documenting all the big and small God moments and blessings.

Keep a sense of humor.

I do realize humor is part of my natural style. But even if laughter does not come naturally for you, even when your life is hard, pray and ask the Lord to find a way in the midst of your pain to make a space for some joy and laughter in your life.

When I first met two Muslim girls that we gave driving lessons to, I was taken with their courage. You cannot imagine the horrors they have lived through. Unfortunately, many of their loved ones did not make it out safely. The first day I met M, I asked if she would be interested in SUP (stand-up paddle boarding) that summer with me. I encouraged her it would be fun, and although my skill level may have been low, my enthusiasm was very high. And that was really all she needed.[5]

It became a bit of joke between us. She told me I was the Queen of Enthusiasm and that we should start a club. A month went by before I was able to visit her again. She told me that she thought about me often, and when she would get sad or depressed or faced a problem, she would think of me and say to herself, "No, I am not going to let this problem beat me. I will face it with enthusiasm, and I will overcome this." Her comment really amazed me. This girl had been through so much, yet our silly conversation had ministered to her and relieved stress.

There are many benefits of laughter. It relaxes the body, helps build up the immune system, and can even burn calories (who can argue against that?). As Proverbs 17:22 says, "A cheerful heart is good medicine, but a crushed spirit dries up the bones." (NIV) Ladies, none of us can afford to have dry bones—they break way too easily. Let the joy of the Lord be your strength.

Give thanks in all things.

"In the midst of the darkest night of the human soul, Jesus found a way to give thanks. Anyone can thank God for the light. Jesus teaches us to thank God for the night. The grateful heart is like a magnet sweeping over the day collecting reasons for gratitude."[6] I love that word picture. You can always find something to be thankful for.

I shared with you how my thankful starting point was being grateful for toilet paper. Now that I spend much of my time in a country that has me in places without it, I truly do find it to be a gift. When I am in the U.S., I get to have clean tap water. Praise God! I feel spoiled beyond what I deserve.

"Enter his gates with thanksgiving; go into his courts with praise. Give thanks to him and praise his name." (Psalm 100:4) The Word tells us the key to the gate into the Lord's presence is thanksgiving. When you have the Lord's presence, you can make it through anything. So get out your magnet sweeper and start today collecting all the things you are thankful for. Write them down and post them on your fridge, bathroom mirror, the dashboard of your car. Wherever it will remind you that you are blessed. Nothing is too small to thank God for.

While I wait to be healed of my migraines, I praise God for medicine, ice packs, and eye masks that block the light from my eyes. Life can be hard. Not denying that. The Word tells us it will be. With God's presence, I can make it through such trials.

Remind yourself that this will not last forever.

Your current situation is not the end. If you are a follower of Jesus, I can promise you that your life has an *amazing* ending. When this life ends, it is the beginning of eternity with Jesus.

Corrie Ten Boom has always been one of my heroes. I could go on and on about why, but I wouldn't want to deprive you of the excitement of discovering the depths of faith from which she lived her life. If you haven't already read about her life in *The Hiding Place*, I wouldn't be offended if you put this book down right now and go find a copy. Well worth it. She was put in a German death camp in World War II for helping to hide Jews. She was the only one in her family to survive the camp. Even though she found herself in the closest thing to hell on earth, she still chose to live her life from a place of victory. Oh, help us, Jesus, to live our life from a "victory is the final outcome" perspective.

Corrie learned her great faith from her father, who before dying in camp, told fellow prisoners that should he be released from the camp that day, he would go right back to helping the Jewish people. His favorite quote was, "The best is yet to come. Whatever comes to pass, heaven awaits us."[7]

Be careful of the conversation you are having with yourself.

What you say to yourself matters! Greatly. Pay attention to what you say.

"We destroy every proud obstacle that keeps people from knowing God. We capture their rebellious thoughts and teach them to obey Christ." (2 Corinthians 10:5)

When I was at my lowest, I remember telling myself, "I can't do this." The Lord corrected me, telling me to stop talking to myself that way. I switched that sentence to Philippians 4:13: "For I can do everything through Christ, who gives me strength." I immediately felt a shift in my emotional well-being.

Negative self-talk produces nothing positive in your life. Cut if off and kick it out just like you would an intruder trying to hurt your children. Those thoughts in your head are trying to hurt God's precious child—you! Memorize that verse, write it on your hand, keep it as your screen saver, write it on a note, and keep it in your pocket. Whatever it takes.

Take one day at a time.

What will usually sink my emotional boat is obsessing over how I will handle the future and all of the possible different scenarios it might bring.

I wrote this in my journal at the airport two weeks before we left for our Iraq trip.

*Sitting back in the airport, I was just talking to the Lord. I feel
like when the day arrives, Lord, will I really have the strength and
peace to step onto the plane? I felt like the Lord told me, "You are
because you are going to take one step at a time. Don't focus on
the end destination. On the 17th, you don't have to go to Iraq;
you just have to fly to Dallas." I can do that, no problem. On the
18th, I still don't have to go to Iraq; I just have to fly to Dubai.
And then I pictured God waiting for me at the airport in Iraq. He
will be waiting for me with the provision I need. For some reason,
it felt more doable when I looked at it that way. I know this is
such a simplistic concept. But I have a way of getting
overwhelmed trying to see the whole picture at once. I'm going to
guess I'm not the only one.*

During our marriage trials, as soon as I started to try and figure out
every detail of every possible outcome of our marriage, I would instantly
become overwhelmed. The Lord encouraged me to just take one step at a
time by not focusing on needing to see the whole finished picture. So I
followed this old saying of "when eating an elephant, eat one bite at a
time." So whether you are trying to get the courage to get on a plane to
be obedient to Christ, or putting up boundaries for a spouse, whatever
your current struggle, try and break it down into small, doable steps.
Sometimes it is just making it through the next five minutes. And then
the next five. And that is completely OK.

*Refuse to stare at the wind and the waves, and lock your eyes on
Jesus.*

"So Peter went over the side of the boat and walked on the water toward
Jesus. But when he saw the strong wind and the waves, he was terrified
and began to sink. "'Save me, Lord!'" he shouted." (Matthew 14:29–30)

In the early stages of preparing for Iraq, I kept reading the news of
what was happening there every day, several times a day. As if more
information on what the enemy was doing there would somehow bring
me peace.

Like I said, I can be slow at times, but the Lord is always gracious with me. The last article I read was how they had to shut down the airport we were to land in due to Russian missiles flying into Syria. I asked the Lord to please help me have peace. I felt the Lord respond to me, "Then stop watching what the enemy is up to, and watch what I am up to instead." From that day on, I banned myself from watching any more news on what ISIS was doing in Iraq.

I know this can be hard, sweet sister, but stop obsessing on what the enemy is doing in your husband's life. Are you consumed and obsessed with checking your husband's emails and text messages—as if a minute-by-minute update will give you peace?

We are not to be naïve in what the enemy is doing, but peace is never found in nervous obsession. Like Peter focusing on the waves, like I was in preparing for Iraq, and like wives obsessing over their husband's communication, focusing on the "waves" of life never results in peace and victory. Only having your eyes locked on Jesus can provide that.

If the Lord could take this girl, who was scared to go on a cruise ship to Mexico, to Iraq at the height of ISIS, and give her peace, then he will do the same for you. The peace came while eating dinner on a patio our first night there, listening to the noise of thunder, which turned out to be bombs. This girl who spent so much of her life scared of everything had peace with bombs going off. I turned to Gina who had talked me through many anxiety nights in the 9/11 year and said, "Can you believe it? We are sitting in Iraq, bombs are going off, and I have peace!"

Isaiah 26:3: "You will keep in perfect peace all who trust in you, all whose thoughts are fixed on you!"

No matter how tough life gets, that's not how it ends. At the end of it all, I get to be with Jesus. And never forget that. You'll be with Jesus—that's your ultimate ending.

Oh, sweet Jesus, please help my dear sisters live every day in this truth. May they not let the opinion of man keep them from experiencing the joy of your presence now and the great anticipation of one day being face-to-face with you. In Jesus's name, I pray for my sweet sisters. Amen.

20

———————————

CONCLUSION

OUR TIME IS COMING to an end. At least for now it is. How do I end this long coffee date?

You may have been wanting a five-point plan on how to change your husband or deliver you from whatever problem you might be facing. I know that is part of the reason I despaired years ago. I always say the main version of my testimony is 2 Corinthians 1:8–11. I have always felt like it describes what the Lord did for me. So when I share my testimony and read this Scripture, I read it this way, because it is very personal to me:

> [I was] crushed and overwhelmed beyond [my] ability to endure, and [I] thought we would never live through it. In fact, [I] expected to die. But as a result, [I] stopped relying on [myself] and learned to rely only on God, who raises the dead. And he did rescue [me] from mortal danger, and he will rescue [me] again. [I] have placed [my] confidence in him, and he will continue to rescue [me]. And you are helping [me] by praying for [me]. Then many people will give thanks because God has graciously answered so many prayers for [my] safety. (2 Corinthians 1:8a–11, additions mine)

Many people have prayed for me and our marriage over the years. I will be forever grateful for a debt I can never repay. If there be anything good in me, it is the result of the undeserved mercy and grace of Jesus in my life. I really don't know what I am doing most of the time other than trusting that Jesus can complete a good work in his "special" daughter. I don't know what our future holds for us, our marriage, or our children. I'm just trusting Jesus to hold it all together because I know I don't have the strength to.

If I have given you the impression our marriage is now perfect, please erase that from your mind because it's not. We still have our family struggles. When either one of us isn't keeping it tight with Jesus, we both can be tempted to fall back into old habits or want to try and hide the times we fail because of fearing what people will think or of potentially losing ministry opportunities. By God's grace so far, we have been able to overcome that temptation. Like every other woman, I still have to trust Jesus for my marriage and ministry. The good news is when these things do arise, they don't instantly steal my peace like it used to.

During a time of working in Iraq, we had a couple of family situations come up—the kind that used to send me into a tailspin. The State Department also issued an evacuation order due to terrorist and potential kidnapping threats. Some people left and some stayed. Everyone had to pray and do what they felt God wanted them to do. We decided to stay. Here is the amazing part. I had peace. Not because I'm awesome but because Jesus is awesome at his job of being the Giver of peace. I told a fellow worker, "You have no idea how cool this is. I once ended up in urgent care because of debilitating fear. I asked Jesus that day, many years ago, if he was who he said he was, then I wanted him to show me how to have peace when my life is not peaceful." I never imagined he would answer that prayer so completely.

God really did do more than I could have ever hoped for or imagined. I am married to one of the godliest men I have ever met. Those who have been forgiven much tend to love much, according to Jesus. I happen to agree. I remember thinking my heart would never completely heal until heaven. I used to picture my heart looking like the smoker lungs they would show you in health class that would be covered with black spots. I felt mostly healed but always felt there were just a couple of residual black spots that wouldn't heal until face-to-face with Jesus. I was OK with that: 95% healed wasn't so bad. That was until Scott went temporarily blind.

When my husband lost his sight, he continually praised Jesus despite his circumstances. I would catch him sitting in a room, completely blind, singing, "Great is your faithfulness." He would sing while leaving the doctor's office, "This little light of mine, I'm going to let it shine." It was like being married to Jesus. Well, almost. The only time I teased him that he was un-Christlike was when he wouldn't go Black Friday shopping with my daughter and me. His red-and-white long cane had the power to part the sea of people. We had a code word for when we wanted him to swing it far and wide. What should have been a scary time of not knowing if my husband would ever see again turned into a precious time of laughing and trusting God in all things.

I've met a lot of women who ask what I do with the flashbacks. I compare it to how I learned to overcome my panic attacks. Hopefully this will make sense to you, but I learned not to fear fear. It's OK. When I feel fear coming on, I have learned to remind myself, *It's no big deal. It will pass. It always does.* Allowing the fear to consume me could negatively affect how I live out Jesus's call on my life.

We had just returned from a weekend with a leadership team for an underground church ministry in another country. One of the men who traveled with one of the underground church pastors told a story of how fear can halt ministry. After a church meeting, back at the hotel, he told the pastor how a man wanted to meet with them. The pastor jumped up, zipped up his jacket, and said, "Where is the church meeting?" His interpreter/travel partner said, "No, it's at the police station." The man who wanted to meet with this pastor was the police chief of the area and wanted a chance to meet them.

Even though they were meeting in a country where there was no real threat to him, the pastor instantly unzipped his jacket and sat back down on the couch. "Tell him sorry. I don't go to police stations." He had spent a lot of time in a prison where he had been tortured. He wanted nothing to do with something that represented the hardest time of his life, even though he saw great provision and miracles take place there.

For some reason one night, when I felt my heart start to race and felt fear creeping in, I started to get frustrated with myself. I felt my Father in heaven comfort me with that story. I pictured this extremely brave pastor who went to very dangerous countries. He had lived and endured so much. He was a powerhouse for the Lord. Even though he had nothing to fear that night by going to the police station, he unzipped his jacket and sat back down on the couch. The police station brought back a lot of traumatic memories.

Please know I'm not trying to compare pain here. It was just a sweet moment the Lord used to encourage me, saying even the ones that you consider to be the bravest can, due to past traumatic memories, decide to unzip the jacket and take a seat and say, "I'm not going there." And that is OK. It's just not OK to live there full time!

I want to encourage you to take time to grieve your losses and seek godly counsel to get healthy, but I encourage you to only set up a temporary tent there. Don't build your permanent housing there. Your life is so much more than your husband's or ex-husband's addictions. Get healthy and come meet me out in the field. There is a world of lost souls that are headed for eternity absent of Christ. Let's not spend our whole lives in the hospitals but get back to the battlefield. Time is ticking.

I realize some of you might not be fortunate to get the same ending as I have. Please always remember true victory is not necessarily a saved marriage but obedience to Christ. That is the only thing we can control.

Yet I do know what awaits me at the end of this earthly life and for you too, if you have trusted your life in the caring hands of Jesus. Revelation 21:3–5 awaits you and me!

> I heard a loud shout from the throne, saying, "Look, God's home
> is now among his people! He will live with them, and they will be
> his people. God himself will be with them. He will wipe every
> tear from their eyes, and there will be no more death or sorrow or

crying or pain. All these things are gone forever." And the one sitting on the throne said, "Look, I am making everything new!" And then he said to me, "Write this down, for what I tell you is trustworthy and true."

And that, my friend, is one GREAT ending!

NOTES

1. Obedience

1. For more information about Gideon's fleece, read Judges 6.

2. Going Back for Others

1. Franklin D. Roosevelt, "Quotable Quote," Goodreads, accessed June 5, 2022, https://www.goodreads.com/quotes/172689-courage-is-not-the-absence-of-fear-but-rather-the.

3. Is Porn a Big Deal?

1. Women's Congregational Policy Institute, Senate Subcommittee Examines Pornography Addiction, accessed October 26, 2020, https://www.w-cpinst.org/source/senate-subcommittee-examines-pornography-addiction/.
2. For more information and resources on the effects of porn and resources, go to puredesire.org.
3. Allison Pearson, "How Online Porn Is Warping Boys' Behaviour with Girls," *The Canberra Times*, April 27, 2015, http://www.canberratimes.com.au/comment/how-online-porn-is-warping-the-behaviour-of-boys-with-girls-20150423-1ms7jw.
4. Melinda Tankard Reist, "What No One Wants to Talk About: How Girls' Bodies Are Injured by Porn Using Boys," April 26, 2015, http://melindatankardreist.com/2015/04/what-no-one-wants-to-talk-about-how-girls-bodies-are-injured-by-porn-using-boys. Used by permission.
5. J. Lee Grady, *Ten Lies the Church Tells Women: How the Bible Has Been Misused to Keep Women in Spiritual Bondage* (Lake Mary, FL: Charisma House, 2006).
6. Ted Roberts, *Conquer Series* (Troutdale, OR: Pure Desire Ministries). Used by permission.
7. Dennis Thompson, "Study Sees Link between Porn, Sexual Dysfunction in Men," *Chicago Tribune*, May 16, 2017, https://www.chicagotribune.com/lifestyles/health/sc-porn-linked-to-sexual-dysfunction-health-0531-20170516-story.html.
8. Robert Weiss, "All about Porn-Induced Erectile Dysfunction," *Huffington Post*, updated February 12, 2017, https://www.huffingtonpost.com/robert-weiss/all-about-porninduced-ere_b_9220706.html.
9. Weiss, "All about Porn-Induced Erectile Dysfunction."

10. "The Porn Industry's Dark Secrets," updated August 23, 2017, *Fight the New Drug* (blog), https://fightthenewdrug.org/the-porn-industrys-dark-secrets.

11. Brandon Griggs, "Terry Crews: Porn Addiction 'Messed Up My Life,'" CNN Entertainment, updated February 24, 2016, https://www.cnn.com/2016/02/24/entertainment/terry-crews-porn-addition-feat/index.html.

4. Growing Up

1. J. M. Barrie, "Wise Old Sayings," accessed October 20, 2020, https://www.wiseoldsayings.com/growing-up-quotes/#ixzz6VmwskoSc.

6. Early Years of Marriage

1. The One Year Bible is divided into daily readings and includes passages from the Old and New Testaments, Psalms, and Proverbs. By the end of the year, you will have read the entire Bible.

2. I feel like an old lady trying to describe life before the invention of the telephone, or in my case, the internet: 900 phone numbers represented being able to call women who were strangers, and they would talk sex. Basically, verbal porn charged by the minute.

7. The Towers Came Down

1. The fire gear that firemen wear for house fires.

2. See John 3:19–21 and Ephesians 5:13.

3. *The Hiding Place* is a book written by Corrie ten Boom about hiding Jews and aiding the Dutch Resistance in WWII.

4. See 2 Corinthians 10:3–5.

5. See Jeremiah 29:11.

6. Crosswalk, "40 Powerful Quotes from Corrie Ten Boom," accessed June 1, 2022, https://www.crosswalk.com/faith/spiritual-life/inspiring-quotes/40-powerful-quotes-from-corrie-ten-boom.html.

7. Hans Poley, *Return to the Hiding Place* (Elgin, IL: Chariot Family Publishers, 1993).

8. My Darkest Night

1. D. C. Talk and The Voice of the Martyrs, *Jesus Freaks: Stories of Those Who Stood for Jesus, the Ultimate Jesus Freaks* (Tulsa, OK: Albury, 1999), 109–110.

2. *Nelson's Illustrated Bible Dictionary*, s.v. "meekness" (Nashville, TN: Thomas Nelson Inc., 1986).

3. *Nelson's Illustrated Bible Dictionary*, s.v. "meekness."

4. Eugene Bach, *Jesus in Iran* (Lumberton, MS: Back to Jerusalem, 2015), 14. Used by permission.

9. Beautiful Breakdown

1. Brother Yun with Paul Hattaway, *The Heavenly Man: The Remarkable True Story of Chinese Christian Brother Yun* (Grand Rapids, MI: Kregel, 2002), 154. Used by permission.

10. Let's Talk Boundaries

1. See John 7:3, John 9:22, and John 12:42.
2. Diane Roberts, *Betrayal and Beyond* (Troutdale, OR: Pure Desire Ministries International, 2013).

11. Discovery

1. James Dobson, *Love Must Be Tough: New Hope for Marriages in Crisis* (Carol Stream, IL: Tyndale Momentum, 2007).
2. Marsha Means, *Living with Your Husband's Secret Wars* (Ada, MI: Revell, 1999). Used by permission.
3. Debbie Laaser, *Faithful and True*, quoted in Marsha Means, *Living with Your Husband's Secret Wars* (Ada, MI: Revell, 1999), 141.
4. Dobson, *Love Must Be Tough*.
5. Gary Thomas, "What You Need to Change When Your Spouse Doesn't," February 27, 2016, *Closer to Christ. Closer to Others* (blog), http://www.gary-thomas.com/what-you-need-to-change-when-your-spouse-doesnt/.
6. If you have access to godly counselors in your area, please take advantage of that. "So don't go to war without wise guidance; victory depends on having many advisers" (Proverbs 24:6). "Plans succeed through good counsel; don't go to war without wise advice" (Proverbs 20:18). "Where there is no guidance the people fall, but in an abundance of counselors there is victory" (Proverbs 11:14, NASB). There are so many Scriptures on the importance of wise counsel; it definitely applies when there is a battle going on for the survival of your family.
7. See Psalm 3:3.

12. My Boundaries

1. Zig Ziglar, *Courtship After Marriage*, series of cassette tapes.
2. See 1 Peter 3. David also did this for Saul in 1 Samuel 24, remaining respectful of the position, but not submitting to abusive behavior.
3. Thomas, "What You Need to Change."

4. That's my term for a wife trying to be a helper, like Eve was Adam's wife *and* helper.

13. Freedom Day

1. Nik Ripkin, *The Insanity of God: A True Story of Faith Resurrected* (Nashville, TN: B&H Books, 2013), 223. Copyright © 2013 by Nik Ripken. All rights reserved. Reprinted and used by permission. It's an amazing book about stories from the persecuted church around the world. Seriously, go buy a copy. You might as well. I'm going to keep referencing it. It's that good.

14. Revelation Day

1. For more information, see *Pure Desire* by Ted Roberts, puredesire.org.
2. Roberts, *Betrayal and Beyond.*
3. Roberts, *Betrayal and Beyond.*

16. Rejection or Protection?

1. Brother Andrew with John and Elizabeth Sherrill, *God's Smuggler* (Bloomington, MI: Chosen Books, 2015).

17. God's Healing

1. For more information and resources on the effects of porn, visit Pure Desire Ministries at puredesire.org.
2. For a copy of the *Betrayal and Beyond* workbook, visit Pure Desire Ministries at puredesire.org.
3. Max Lucado, *Before Amen: The Power of a Simple Prayer* (Nashville, TN: Thomas Nelson, 2014).
4. If your husband is not repentant or in a right frame of mind to be an asset in your healing, please seek out a godly counselor or pray for the Lord to lead you to a woman who has already walked this path in a healthy, godly way to help you on your journey. You are not meant to walk through it alone.

18. Submission

1. Ravi Zacharias and Dennis Prager, "The Death of Truth, The Decline of Culture Q&A," YouTube video, 1:13:07, January 1, 2018, https://www.youtube.com/watch?v=lcAP4Be9LZQ.
2. Zacharias and Prager, "The Death of Truth."

3. Dennis Prager, "There Is a 'Worst' Sin: Evil in God's Name," *National Review*, December 23, 2014, http://www.nationalreview.com/article/395265/there-worst-sin-evil-gods-name-dennis-prager.

4. One Year Bible, Commentary (Carol Stream, IL: Tyndale House Publishers, Inc., 2007).

5. I'm not condoning purposefully bad mouthing your husband for revenge or bringing harm to him. Always remember God cares about motives.

6. Ripkin, *The Insanity of God*, 252.

19. Battle Plan

1. Ripkin, *The Insanity of God*, 181.

2. Max Lucado, *You'll Get through This: Hope and Help for Your Turbulent Times* (Nashville, TN: Thomas Nelson, 2015).

3. L. B. Cowman, *Streams in the Desert* (Grand Rapids, MI: Zondervan), 43.

4. *The Cross and the Switchblade* by David Wilkerson, John Sherrill, and Elizabeth Sherrill. *The Heavenly Man* by Brother Yun and Paul Hattaway.

5. Enthusiasm plus a life jacket! The majority of my Muslim ladies can't swim, but that doesn't stop us. I life-jacket them up—hijab and all!

6. Max Lucado, *You'll Get through This*.

7. Corrie ten Boom, *A Prisoner and Yet* (CLC Publications, 1980).

ABOUT THE AUTHOR

Anna Luke is an experienced speaker at numerous churches and women's events, drawing upon her great sense of humor and storytelling abilities. She has often been described by attendees as genuine and down to earth. Anna has a heart for the hurting and works with the refugee community in her area. She is also a global advocate for abused women and has helped women who have been trafficked to the Middle East.

Anna acknowledges that it is nothing but the grace of God she is where she is today, a woman healed of debilitating panic attacks and passionate to always say yes to Jesus, even if it sounds crazy.

Contact me at authorannaluke@gmail.com

www.ingramcontent.com/pod-product-compliance
Lightning Source LLC
Chambersburg PA
CBHW071507140726
47997CB00005B/1890